Cinema, Censorship and Sexuality, 1909–1925

Cinema and Society

General Editor

Jeffrey Richards
Department of History
University of Lancaster

Also available in this series:

Mass Observation at the Movies
Jeffrey Richards and Dorothy Sheridan

Cinema, Censorship and Sexuality, 1909–1925

Annette Kuhn

Routledge

London and New York

First published in 1988 by
Routledge
11 New Fetter Lane, London EC4P 4EE

Published in the USA by
Routledge Inc.
in association with Methuen Inc.
29 West 35th Street, New York, NY 10001

Set in 9/12 pt Century
by Input Typesetting Ltd, London
and printed in Great Britain
by TJ Press (Padstow) Ltd
Padstow, Cornwall

Library of Congress Cataloging in Publication Data

British Library CIP Data also available

ISBN 0–415–00381–4

Dedicated to
the memory of my father,
Henry Philip Kuhn

Contents

List of Illustrations

General Editor's Preface

The pre-eminent popular art form of the first half of the twentieth century has been the cinema. Both in Europe and America from the turn of the century to the 1950s cinema-going has been a regular habit and film-making a major industry. The cinema combined all the other art forms – painting, sculpture, music, the word, the dance – and added a new dimension – an illusion of life. Living, breathing people enacted dramas before the gaze of the audience and not, as in the theatre, bounded by the stage, but with the world as their backdrop. Success at the box office was to be obtained by giving the people something to which they could relate and which therefore reflected themselves. Like the other popular art forms, the cinema has much to tell us about people and their beliefs, their assumptions and their attitudes, their hopes and fears and dreams.

This series of books will examine the connection between films and the societies which produced them. Film as straight historical evidence; film as an unconscious reflection of national preoccupations; film as escapist entertainment; film as a weapon of propaganda – these are the aspects of the question that will concern us. We shall seek to examine and delineate individual film *genres*, the cinematic images of particular nations and the work of key directors who have mirrored national concerns and ideals. For we believe that the rich and multifarious products of the cinema constitute a still largely untapped source of knowledge about the ways in which our world and the people in it have changed since the first flickering images were projected on to the silver screen.

Jeffrey Richards

Acknowledgments

This book started life as a PhD thesis, research for which was made possible by funding from the Economic and Social Research Council. The University of London Institute of Education also provided various forms of support, material and otherwise; and the Australian National University made available facilities which permitted completion of the project's writing up.

Viewings of films were made possible by the National Film Archive; the Motion Picture, Broadcasting and Recorded Sound Division of the Library of Congress; David Samuelson; Kevin Brownlow; and Bob Geoghegan of the Archive Film Agency. For their assistance in tracking down documents, I am obliged to the staffs of the Public Record Office, the Fawcett Library, the Department of Manuscripts at the British Library, the Information Department of the British Film Institute; and especially to Barbara Hall of the Margaret Herrick Library at the Academy of Motion Picture Arts and Sciences, and Barbara Humphrey at the Library of Congress. Film historians Mary Beth Haralovich and Richard Maltby were generous with information on archival sources in the US, and Harold Dunham offered helpful background details on the Samuelson films discussed in chapters 4 and 5.

Jane Caplan, Philip Corrigan, Philip Drummond, John Hayes and Jill Julius Matthews gave advice on the conduct of the inquiry, or read and commented upon various written drafts; and Basil Bernstein came up with encouragement and practical assistance when it was most needed. In turning the thesis into a book, I have been much encouraged by Jeffrey Weeks and Jeffrey Richards. None of the individuals who helped in these ways are to be held responsible for the shortcomings of the final product, however. The University of London Library provided me with a quiet place to work; so, at a particularly difficult time, did my friends Diana Woodward and Jean Glasscock of Sheffield, and Brodnax Moore and Annie Fatet of Hebden Bridge.

Work-in-progress on the project has been presented at the Annual Conference of the British Sociological Association, Cardiff, April 1983; at the Annual Meeting of the Society for Cinema Studies, New York University, June 1985; and at the Power Foundation, Sydney University, June 1986. Earlier versions of chapters 4 and 5 have been published respectively in *The Power of the Image: Essays on Representation and Sexuality* (London: Routledge & Kegan Paul, 1985); and in *Screen*, vol. 27, no. 2 (1986). Extracts from Crown-copyright records in the Public Record Office appear

xiv   ACKNOWLEDGMENTS

by permission of Her Majesty's Stationery Office. The picture of Lois Weber
at work was supplied by the National Film Archive; and stills – produced
by Jim Adams – from Samuelson films appear courtesy of the Samuelson
Family Archive.

Annette Kuhn
London, May 1987

Abbreviations

BBFC	British Board of Film Censors
BSHC	British Social Hygiene Council
CEA	Cinematograph Exhibitors' Association
LCC	London County Council
MCC	Middlesex County Council
NCCVD	National Council for Combating Venereal Disease
NCPM	National Council of Public Morals
NVA	National Vigilance Association

Investigating Film Censorship

I try to study the play and development of a set of diverse realities articulated on to each other.

Michel Foucault, 1981

Questions of censorship

The title of this book suggests a rather diverse set of concerns. But the point of entry for this inquiry into cinema, censorship and sexuality is quite specific: the story begins with the birth of film censorship in Britain. It proceeds eventually to a consideration of how institutions and practices of film censorship were involved in the constitution of cinema as a public sphere of regulation. Along the way, institutions, discourses and practices which might at first sight appear to have little or nothing to do with the censorship of films are drawn into the investigation. And in the process, the concept of censorship itself is subjected to critical scrutiny and redefinition.

My inquiry has a quite limited time frame, in that it focuses on the years between 1909 and 1925. Periodisations of this sort can be misleading in their promise of precision, for historical events are rarely capable of being pinned down temporally to exact beginnings and ends, but in the present case there are a number of arguments in favour of this strategy. In 1909 the Cinematograph Act, the earliest British legislation relating specifically to cinema, entered the statute book. Although not originally framed as a censorship measure, the Cinematograph Act soon came to constitute the legal underpinning of a variety of film censorship practices. Its passage can thus be considered a key moment in the history of film censorship in Britain. While the year 1925 may offer no such clear mark of transition, it is taken as the endpoint of investigation because the various institutions and practices which were to govern the subsequent conduct of British film censorship were not really in place until the mid-1920s.

The years between 1909 and 1925 are important because they constitute a period of uncertainty – even of struggle – over the means by which cinema was to be understood, defined and regulated. The entire period, in fact, may be regarded as an extended moment of risk. During these years not only were the forces at work in film censorship more exposed, more in danger, than they would ever afterwards be, but the institution of cinema was itself in process of becoming. As an industry, cinema was beginning to establish itself as a social and economic force to be reckoned with; while as a form of representation it was developing conventions which would privilege highly specific approaches to cinematic narration and ultimately secure lasting dominance for the fiction feature film.

In taking film censorship in Britain as a point of departure, this study draws on other work on the subject. In the end, though, it constructs its object – censorship – rather differently. Existing studies of censorship tend to be dominated by what I shall call a 'prohibition/institutions' model. Within this frame of reference, censorship is understood first and foremost as an act of prohibition, excision, or 'cutting-out' – a practice through which certain subjects are forbidden expression in representations. Debates on censorship, both pro- and anti-, invariably see it as a prohibitive process, assuming that a censored text, by distorting 'reality' or in some other sense falling short of it, is in some sense partial in its representation.

This view is grounded in a distinction between a 'real' world of social action on the one hand, and texts and representations on the other. It assumes, moreover, that the 'real' constitutes a kind of self-evident truth, a truth that should – or in certain circumstances should not – be reflected in representations; and that censorship stands, rightly or wrongly, in the way of this process of reflection. All this assumes a subordination of representation to 'reality', some consequences of which will be explored later in this chapter.

At this point, though, I shall simply note that the prohibition model constructs censorship as a *problem* of a certain kind: a problem, basically, of 'interference'. This interference seems automatically to demand either justification or condemnation. This approach characterises a substantial body of writing on censorship and cinema, from the early arguments against the political censorship of films put forward in Dorothy Knowles's book *The Censor, the Drama and the Film*, through arguments advanced in the 1970s by the Festival of Light in favour of tighter moral censorship, to libertarian counterarguments by the likes of John Trevelyan, film censor during the 'permissive' 1960s, and the more recent equivocations of the Williams Committee in its report on obscenity and film censorship.[1]

The question at the centre of all of these studies, however, is the extent to which prohibitions on the content of films constitute a justifiable exercise of power in a 'free' society. The prohibitive power at issue might be held by the state or by other bodies holding claims to legitimate authority, but whatever its source, the power at stake in the prohibition model of censorship is always exactly a power of repression, of 'no-saying'. To question this model is by no means to deny that censorship has anything to do with power. On the contrary, what I want to suggest in fact is that an understanding of power as a purely prohibitive gesture – especially where the object of prohibition is taken to be the representation of some pre-existing reality – does not go far enough, and may actually inhibit our understanding of how, and with what effects, the powers involved in film censorship work.

The prohibition model of censorship is usually associated with a further assumption: that censorship is something that takes place within certain organisations, especially in organisations with an explicit institutional remit to censor. This composite is the 'prohibition/institutions' model, which constructs censorship as an activity guided by practices of exclusion, and locates those practices in organisations such as boards of film censors, or in institutions whose activities impinge directly upon those of censorship bodies. Among the latter, the law and the film industry have figured most prominently in the literature on film censorship. Accounts of film censorship in Britain as it has affected (and sometimes from the point of view of) the film trade appear, for example, in a number of general histories of British cinema,[2] while the involvement of laws and legal institutions in the censorship of films is dealt with historically, comparatively and authoritatively by Neville March Hunnings in his book *Film Censors and the Law*.[3]

But if any coherent body of work on film censorship in Britain – as opposed, that is, to brief surveys and isolated, if influential, studies of the subject – can be identified, it takes the form of a set of studies in political history which deal primarily with censorship organisations, and with the British Board of Film Censors in particular. This work includes accounts of the political complexion of British governments of the 1930s and how it is reflected in film censorship practices of the period, of film censorship during World War II and its relation to government policies on wartime propaganda, of the hegemony of the British establishment as expressed in film censorship during the 1930s, and of the history of the British Board of Film Censors from its inception until 1950.[4] As a body of work, it concerns itself with political as opposed to moral censorship, and discusses censorship as an effect of the policies and interests of various British governments. In assuming that film censorship is basically an activity of a specific censorship organisation, subject in whatever degree to government pressure, it operates an institutional model of censorship. And to the extent that it regards the British Board of Film Censors as an agency of exclusion or limitation, it is grounded in a prohibition model.

In understanding censorship as a prohibitive activity on the part of a self-contained and predefined set of institutions, the prohibition/institutions model takes censorship as a given, and reifies it. If this model provides a certain purchase on the historical study of film censorship, this is only because it constructs, *a priori*, an object of inquiry which is relatively amenable to empirical investigation. By the same token, though, the definition of censorship which both emerges from and sustains the prohibition/ institutions model is a constricting one, for it allows only one story – and not necessarily the most interesting or important one – to be told about film censorship.

The prohibition/institutions model effects a prior limitation of its object – censorship – with several significant consequences. First of all, the focus on concrete institutions – even where these are not confined to censorship bodies – *isolates* censorship practices from their broader social and historical conditions of existence and effectivity. Second, to assume that censorship only prohibits or represses is to forget that censorship might equally well be *productive* in its effects. Finally, although the prohibition/ institutions model does permit the question of *power* to enter into considerations of censorship, the negative, institution-based power it assumes is overly static and univocally deterministic.

Text, context, apparatus

In studies of censorship and cinema, the shortcomings of the prohibition/ institutions model are nowhere more evident than when it comes to looking at films. This is particularly true as regards the question of power, for the prohibition/institutions model constructs film censorship basically as a one-way street, something that is *done to* films. Within this perspective, films are seen as caught up in institutions which already possess the power to determine their character or their content through the deployment of pre-existing prohibitions. Films, given such assumptions, are constructed as merely inert, passive objects.

In other words, in the prohibition/institutions model films are seen as subordinate to laws, rules and procedures of censorship, and to the structure and organisation of censor boards and other institutions. While individual films are often discussed, sometimes at length, in this context, their status invariably remains secondary. At the very most, legal actions or other controversies over particular films might be treated as heralding reforms in censorship laws, or as challenging government policies.[5] At work in the prohibition/institutions model and its subordination of the film text, therefore, is a determinism which holds that films are shaped by institutional practices and can be seen only in terms of their absences, of what has been actively denied expression in them.

Governing as they do historical studies of film censorship, these assumptions form part of a more extensive discursive strategy, a strategy which constructs the intellectual field of film history and governs the conduct of inquiries into the history of cinema. This is an insistence upon a separation between social structures and institutions on the one hand and representations on the other, with a concomitant subordination of the latter to the former.[6] This in turn produces a dichotomy which structures the entire field of film studies: the dualism of text and context. The text-context dualism constitutes film texts and the social, historical and institutional contexts in which films are produced, distributed and consumed as distinct objects of inquiry, so rendering virtually insurmountable the task of exploring, without recourse to determinism, their interaction.

A whole series of conceptual and methodological consequences sustains, and flows from, the division of texts from contexts. In particular, distinct systems of thought are deployed in the theorisation of each, and their investigation is governed by different methodologies. In studies of cinema, the conceptual realm of the film text is inhabited by semiotics-based criticisms which, taking meaning as their starting point, construct texts as processes of signification, often constituting them, in abstraction from the social, as more or less self-contained objects.[7] The terrain of contexts, on the other hand, is marked out by institutions, social relations and social practices surrounding the production, distribution and exhibition of films; thinking in these areas tends to hold contexts as determining and texts as determined.

Each system distinguishes itself from the other by drawing a line of demarcation between representation and a 'real world' of social practice. This demarcation process works in effect as a policing of boundaries between disciplines and modes of inquiry, and between their respective practitioners: if texts are the province of the semiotician and the critical theorist, then contexts are the property of the social scientist and the historian. But if the study of cinema calls for a crossing of disciplinary boundaries, such divisions are perhaps less easily ignored in film studies than in more established fields of knowledge. And indeed, there have recently been attempts by historians of film to grapple with some of the problems posed by the dualism of text and context. The writers concerned do, however, continue in some measure to accept the basic terms of the dualism,[8] perhaps because, formulated in terms of text and context, a project of redefinition is in the final instance impossible.

For the text-context dualism constructs a conceptual and methodological gulf which is unbridgeable within the terms of any of the systems of thought sustaining it. Nevertheless, since the prohibition/institutions model of film censorship is complicit in the dichotomy of text and context, some attempt to resolve the latter at a methodological level is obviously called for here. But if by resolving the dualism is implied some merging together of text and context, then resolution is clearly not possible: an unravelling, perhaps, or a deconstruction, might be more to the point. If the text-context dichotomy is to be transcended, therefore, we must abandon the dualistic thinking which produced the impasse in the first place.

The nub of the problem is that the text-context dualism proposes a distinction between representations and institutions. Therefore any attempt at a methodological breakthrough must begin with a challenge to this distinction. It might be productive, for instance, to stop regarding representations as objects confined to a 'cultural' realm, and stop seeing institutions as locked into a sphere of the 'real'. Meaning would then be liberated to enter the social, and the social to inhabit meaning, and both to be understood as practices and processes rather than as static objects. This would at least admit a greater fluidity into conceptualisations of relations between practices than is possible in those areas of knowledge sustained by the text-context dualism.

What would be the hallmarks of a historical study of film censorship which sought to free itself of the restrictions imposed in general by the text-context dualism, and in particular by the prohibition/institutions model? Such an inquiry would first of all aim to take into account the conditions of operation and effectivity of film censorship. Under this heading might be included the practices of concrete institutions, among them those devoted to the censorship of films; but such institutions would be seen not in isolation but as both active and acted upon within a wider set of practices and relations. Second, the productive capacity of film censorship, as activated in the interrelations of various practices, would require acknowledgment. Third, the nature of the powers involved in film censorship would be re-examined. And fourth, film texts would be rescued from their subordination to contexts and accorded a place, an instrumentality in their own right, among the various practices which constitute film censorship.

The question for such an inquiry would be not so much what film censorship is, as how it works. The object of inquiry is transformed, then, and censorship ceases to be a reified and predefined object, becoming instead something which emerges from the interactions of certain processes and practices. Censorship, in short, would be seen (to adopt the terminology of Michel Foucault) as part of an apparatus, a *dispositif*,

> a thoroughly heterogeneous ensemble consisting of discourses, institutions, architectural forms, regulatory decisions, laws, administrative measures, scientific statements, philosophical, moral and philanthropic propositions.

An apparatus, according to Foucault, is more than merely the sum total of a series of variegated components. Its most important characteristic is its *activity*, the interactions between its parts – its practices and processes. These interrelations are always fluid, always in a state of becoming, always 'inscribed in a play of power'.[9]

Censorship can be regarded, then, as an activity which participates in an apparatus, in a set of practices whose interrelations are imbued not so much with power *tout court* as with the 'play' of power. Power, in this model, is a process, precisely a holding-in-play,

> a network of relations, constantly in tension, rather than a privilege that one might possess. . . . In short, this power is exercised rather than possessed.[10]

If power is a relationship – or rather a set of relations or field of forces – it is not of itself susceptible to observation, at least in any positivistic sense; nor indeed does it reside in any particular individuals or institutions. Power is all-encompassing, a web that enmeshes the entire field of the social. This notion of power, as Foucauldian terms such as 'network' and 'domain' imply, is usefully understood in spatial and relational terms.[11] But while power might be everywhere, each apparatus embodies a unique configuration, a unique 'network', of powers. The apparatus does not, however, exist prior to its powers. Power, in other words, emerges – it is produced – in specific instances, in concrete sets of relations.

Important among the relations in which power is produced, suggests Foucault, are 'certain co-ordinates of knowledge':

> there is no power relation without the constitution of a field of knowledge, nor any knowledge that does not presuppose at the same time power relations.[12]

Relations of power may operate, therefore, in the service of producing and regulating the 'truth', especially as 'truth' governs the constitution of particular forms of knowledge. In certain circumstances, therefore, power and regulation can be productive, rather than – or as well as – repressive, operations.[13] Regulation, in consequence, may be understood not so much as an imposition of rules upon some preconstituted entity, but as an ongoing and always provisional process of constituting objects from and for its own practices.

Power, so conceptualised, is impossible to pin down to any positive prior definition. It becomes much easier, in fact, to see power in terms of what it is not. Power is not a thing, nor is it located in any particular place; it is not held by specific institutions, nor is it to be regarded as a hidden logic of history. Even such a negative understanding of power offers a challenge to the crudeness and determinism of many existing definitions of the term. The strength of this approach – which permits power to be understood as process, as activity – is that it allows for the conceptualisation of unevenness, resistance, conflict, and ongoing transformation in relations of power. And the notion that power can actually be productive in certain ways subjects to question the widely-held view that it works primarily as a machinery of repression.

But if power relations, thought in this way, can neither be directly observed nor theorised in advance, how can they be investigated? How can something so dynamic and fluid ever be subjected to inquiry? At an abstract or a general level, in fact, it cannot: it has to be seen in operation, for power relations can only be analysed at work in specific social and historical 'instances'. This shift of perspective on power and its operation immediately brings into focus new objects and procedures of inquiry. Above all, as far as the present investigation is concerned, the text-context dualism is not resolved so much as made redundant. Investigation directs itself not at texts or at contexts, nor at organisations and rules of exclusion, but at the nature of the practices, relations and powers involved in film censorship, and at what these produce – their effectivity – at particular moments in history.

In an investigation of this sort, it is unnecessary – indeed it would be counterproductive – to start out with any predefined notion of film censorship, or with assumptions about where censorship takes place and with what outcomes. The task of setting out the terms of inquiry is approached differently: film censorship ceases, in any *a priori* sense, to be the object of investigation. It is replaced instead by a focus upon 'events' or 'instances'. The question for the investigator then becomes: how, where, and with what consequences does censorship emerge from the 'heterogeneous ensemble' of practices and relations which constitute any one instance?

This kind of approach has been termed variously 'causal analysis' and 'eventalisation'. Film historians Robert C. Allen and Douglas Gomery, following Roy Bhaskar, advocate a Realist approach to film history, an approach which consists in a recognition that the object of study is not so much an historical event *per se* as the 'causal mechanisms' that brought it about. Causal analysis involves first of all redescription of the event with a view to uncovering the possible causal mechanisms underlying it, and second, analysis of these mechanisms.[14] This procedure appears to be similar in certain respects to the method termed by Foucault, with reference to his history of the prison, 'eventalisation' or 'causal multiplication'. This 'consists in analysing an event according to the multiple processes which constitute it'.[15]

While for either of these approaches the event itself may be real, its generative mechanisms, its *dispositif*, are not open to direct observation. They are, nevertheless, available for investigation in the sense that they can be uncovered, or recovered, by means of analysis or 'diagnosis'. The starting point of analysis is a 'snapshot', so to speak, of an historical moment, of an instance or set of practices. The web of 'force relations' at work within that instance is then unravelled, and scrutinised in its actual operation.

Events and instances

What is the potential of this kind of approach for the present inquiry, whose starting point is the birth and early years of film censorship in Britain – for a project, that is, whose object is in some sense already defined? As I have argued, the conceptualisation of film censorship brought into focus by the notion of the apparatus brings about a reformulation of the very object of investigation. This is underscored by the strategy of eventalisation and the activity of diagnosis. Film censorship becomes an activity embedded within an ensemble of power relations, whose operation can be unpicked through attention to particular events and instances. Even if the latter might present themselves for investigation in the first place because they appear to involve film censorship in its taken-for-granted sense as an institutional practice of prohibition, the activity of diagnosis reveals that a great deal more than this is at stake.

It is in the nature of this approach that its productivity is not readily demonstrable in advance, emerging only in actual performance. Thus while my inquiry concerns itself with events surrounding the censorship of films in the years between 1909 and 1925, it is centred on a set of three case histories, analyses of historical instances involving censorship. In these instances the powers at work in the censorship of films are not merely observable, but can actually be scrutinised in action. The case history approach offers practical demonstration that discourses, practices, and powers emerge as processes in their instrumentality in concrete historical instances, and can be neither defined nor fixed in any way prior to their operation in such instances.

The case histories are discussed in chapters 3, 4 and 5 of this book. The starting point of each one is a particular film or group of films, all commercial fiction features, British and American, produced between 1909 and 1925. Chapter 3 looks at events surrounding the arrival in Britain of a Hollywood feature film whose story centres on the practice of abortion by an upper-middle-class woman, in chapter 4 a series of fiction films 'about' venereal diseases is discussed, while chapter 5 deals with a narrative film co-written by birth control campaigner Marie Stopes. Each of these films or groups of films became caught up, in different ways, in processes of censorship. And each of the three cases is treated as an 'event' and analysed with the object first of all of revealing the configuration of forces at work in each instance, and ultimately of bringing to light the powers at work across all three instances and over a certain period.

To place film texts at the centre of case histories is not necessarily to imply any determining role or priority for texts in apparatuses of censorship. Rather it is a gesture – in part strategic – of instating films and their textual operations (their organisation of narrative, character, and *mise-en-scène*, for example) as practices which themselves inscribe, transform and produce other discourses and practices. In this inquiry, among the latter may be counted discourses around sex and sexuality. On one level, all the films discussed in this book may be read as dealing with aspects of 'the sexual': abortion, VD, birth control. The sexual, however, does not so much already inhabit the content of these films as become produced in specific ways in the discourses and practices which surround them. Analysis therefore extends itself to the institutions, institutional practices, powers and knowledges which organise the sexual within and beyond these films, and which are involved in their construction as objects of censorship.

The three case histories are preceded, in chapter 2, by a description of developments in film censorship in Britain during the 1909–25 period. The emphasis in this chapter is on institutions – including the British Board of Film Censors, the law, the cinema industry and the Home Office – and their interrelations: a background is sketched in against which may be set the events subsequently analysed in the case histories. The discussion in chapter 2 also adds detail to existing histories, which for the most part deal rather superficially with film censorship in Britain during the period covered by this inquiry. But most important of all, perhaps, chapter 2 begins to engage with the various institutional practices surrounding film censorship in this period – a necessary first step in the task of unravelling the ensemble of powers, practices and discourses constituting the apparatus within which film censorship is embedded.

In the case histories which follow is brought to light a more extensive array of discourses, practices and powers: these, as I shall argue, are implicated not merely in the censorship of films, but more broadly in a series of processes through which cinema was itself to become subject to regulation. These include discourses active earlier this century in producing, circulating and 'applying' knowledges which aspired to order the domain of the sexual in its relation with the social. Chapter 6 looks at cinema's involvement with these knowledges, and at the instrumentality, in discursive constructions of what I shall call the 'socio-sexual', of the films which figure in the case histories. At the same time, certain other practices and powers emerge from the case histories as participating in the more extensive discursive project of producing cinema as a public sphere of regulation. Chapter 7 traces the processes by which a public sphere of cinema became constituted through a series of alliances and conflicts involving – but not confined to – the law, the film trade, film censorship bodies, and organisations devoted to the promotion of public morality and social purity. At the centre of all this activity stood the cinema audience, which inhabited cinema's public sphere mainly as a problem demanding urgent action. The audience was to become a key component of a construction of cinema which sanctioned certain practices of censorship. Cinema, in this sense, was not so much subjected to, as created through, regulation.

Film censorship emerges here as active in its own right in the construction of a public sphere of cinema. It also emerges as a product, for it operates in the space of resistance to various strategies of regulation of cinema's public sphere. Chapter 8 argues that, as well as being at once productive and produced, film censorship is a process embodying complex and potentially contradictory relations of power. From these powers, it is suggested, emerges a public sphere of cinema constituted by particular objects of regulation: modes of consumption of films, consumers of films, categories of films, and last – and quite possibly least – contents of films.

2   The Birth of Film Censorship in Britain

In our strange, illogical, haphazard British way we have established this wholly anomalous institution.

Herbert Samuel, Home Secretary, 1932

The question of institutions

A focus on institutions, as I have noted, does not exhaust the processes and productivities involved in the censorship of films, nor should it be taken to suggest that institutions exist prior to the power relations in which they are implicated. Nevertheless, the activity within these relations of a particular set of institutional practices (which can be termed, for the time being, 'censorship institutions') is significant enough to render some general account of their operation useful to an understanding of events detailed in the three case histories which follow this chapter. Those institutions most obviously involved (at first sight, at least) in film censorship – the film industry, the law, and the British Board of Film Censors – will be examined here. I shall also look at relations between these institutions, and at their interactions with central and local government agencies responsible for matters of film censorship.

In the case histories, institutions other than these emerge as involved in the censorship of films, while the censorship institutions themselves quite often turn out to be operating in mutual contradiction, or to be less instrumental than other institutional practices in the shaping of events. The censorship institutions, then, are not to be regarded as acting in isolation – either from each other, or from other institutional practices. Nor are the former to be seen as necessarily more 'important' than the latter. Whatever institutional practices might be at work, and however they might be at work, in each of the instances unfolded in the case histories, the censorship institutions are in the final instance only part of a larger ensemble of institutions, practices, powers and relations: they participate, in short, in an apparatus.

To describe the operations of the censorship institutions before seeing them in action in specific instances is to run the risk of reifying them. It is perhaps worth repeating, therefore, that none of these institutions pre-exists the powers of censorship they might exercise. On the contrary, they are nothing more than, they exist only in and through, those powers. They are censorship institutions, then, only in their status as historically-specific agglomerations or crystallisations of capacities to exercise powers of particular kinds.[1] The account of certain institutions and institutional practices in this chapter is thus no more than provisional, being simply a first step toward the ultimate goal of uncovering a whole array of powers, practices and discourses governing film censorship at a particular historical moment.

The cinema industry and the law

The first public film show in Britain took place in February 1896, when the Lumière Cinematograph was presented at the Regent Street Polytechnic in London. Thirteen years later, a bill aimed at regulating cinematograph exhibitions, the earliest British legislation touching specifically on cinema, passed through Parliament as the Cinematograph Act 1909, a measure designed 'to make better provision for securing safety at Cinematograph and other Exhibitions'. In the interim, film shows had mostly moved out of music halls (where they had on occasion been slotted between the live acts), out of 'penny gaffs' and fairground sideshows, and into new, purpose-built picture palaces.

In this relatively short period of time, film-going had already become a popular leisure pursuit, and the film trade was beginning to develop into an industry of some substance, with international connections and ever-increasing capitalisation. In 1906, the earliest purpose-built cinemas in Britain had been opened, and the first film trade body – the Kinematograph Manufacturers' Association – formed. Over the following few years, trade organisations representing distributors and exhibitors also came into existence: the Incorporated Association of Film Renters in 1910, and the Cinematograph Exhibitors' Assocation in 1912. During the early 1910s, the cinema industry in Britain underwent a huge expansion, especially on the exhibition side. For instance, while in 1910 there were only three exhibition companies in existence, five years later there were more than 1800. Being responsible between them for some 4000 cinemas, most of these businesses were small: nevertheless, they held combined capital in excess of £11 million. It has been estimated, too, that in 1914 cinema admissions reached around 364 million for the year: a small figure by comparison with the peak admissions of the 1940s, but considerable nonetheless given that only a few years earlier cinemas had scarcely even existed.

The power of the exhibitors grew accordingly: in the year of its inception, the CEA took a prominent part in lobbying the government for a trade-sponsored system of 'voluntary' censorship of films, and several years later succeeded virtually single-handed in forcing it to shelve a scheme of official censorship devised in response to criticisms of the voluntary arrangements. In Britain, though, film production was in a somewhat less robust state than exhibition. Already in 1909 about one-third of all films screened in British cinemas were imports from the USA. Although this proportion fluctuated over the next decade, the trend was in general upward: by the end of World War I, for instance, as many as sixty per cent of films exhibited in Britain were American. After the war, when US distributors succeeded in penetrating the British market, effectively monopolising film bookings, American domination of British cinema screens became virtually complete.

This was a crucial – perhaps indeed the major – precipitating factor in a crisis which hit British film production in the early 1920s: by the mid-1920s, hardly any films were being made and many producers had gone out of business. In an attempt to halt the decline, the Cinematograph Films Act – aimed at fostering local production by ensuring that a certain proportion of screen time would be devoted to British films – was passed in 1927.[2] Thus, during the period covered by this inquiry, cinema in Britain became a booming and increasingly profitable commercialised leisure industry, but its strength lay mainly in marketing, rather than in making, films. In these circumstances, censorship would obviously operate most effectively not at the point of production but at the points of distribution and exhibition. Trade intervention in censorship tended in consequence to come from distributors and exhibitors.

In fact, the film industry's position on censorship fluctuated a good deal in the years between 1909 and 1925. While the 1909 Cinematograph Act was passed with the trade's support, complaints about the implementation of the new law quite soon began to be heard from this quarter; and although film industry organisations were instrumental in setting up the 'voluntary' censorship scheme operated by the British Board of Film Censors, the Board's conduct of censorship also soon became a target of industry criticism. Nevertheless, when the BBFC was on the verge of transformation into an organ of state censorship, the trade fought vigorously to save it.

Throughout all this, the film industry's main concern was usually to maximise audiences, though from time to time other considerations supervened. Exhibitors were particularly unenthusiastic about censorship, regarding it in general as an unwarranted interference in the conduct of business. At the same time, though, the trade as a whole was engaged in a more or less ceaseless quest for respectability, for cinema was widely looked upon as at best a vulgar sideshow, at worst a serious social problem. Because of this, certain sections of it came rather reluctantly to the view that some sort of regulation of films was inevitable, if not desirable. Underlying the trade's initial support of the Cinematograph Act and the BBFC, then, lay an aspiration both to improve cinema's public image, and to avert more stringent forms of censorship.

In this context, the film industry's attitude towards, and use of, the law is worth examining. Before the Cinematograph Act was passed, the new medium of cinema had flourished in a somewhat *laissez-faire* climate, such regulation of film shows as existed being rather uneven. For example, the licensing provisions applicable to music halls and other places of public entertainment in which music or dancing took place covered some, but not all, screenings of films. The Disorderly Houses Act 1751, a measure originally intended to control 'places of entertainment for the lower sort of people', called for the licensing of any premises of this sort within twenty miles of the City of London or Westminster. When the local government system was reformed nationally in 1888, powers to grant licences under this Act were transferred from magistrates to the newly-formed county councils – in this case, given the Act's limited geographical coverage, initially only to the London County Council, though in 1890 the provisions of the Disorderly Houses Act were extended to cover the entire country.

Film shows in premises licensed under this Act were subject to the licensing conditions pertaining in general to such premises, though the LCC soon caught up with the new technology. In 1898, less than two years after the opening of the Lumière films, it issued a set of regulations which applied specifically to cinematograph performances in places of public entertainment already licensed by the Council. These rules reflected current public concern about fires in theatres, and dealt solely with safety precautions, covering matters such as smoking, and the construction and illumination of the cinematograph lantern (the projector).

However, film exhibitions had not, as I have noted, been confined to premises of the sort covered by the Disorderly Houses Act. Fairground sideshows and penny gaffs, for example, fell outside the Act's scope, and when film shows started being mounted more often in purpose-built premises, the limits of this Act were put to the test in a series of court cases. Judgments in these cases suggested that existing legislation did in fact apply to purpose-built cinemas.[3] But if the Disorderly Houses Act gave local authorities powers to determine the conditions under which films were screened, it was rare in this early period for film titles, advertising or content to be covered in licensing regulations. The censorship of films, then, was not at this point an issue with which the law relating to places of public entertainment concerned itself, either directly or indirectly.

This is not to say that there had been no public concern at all before 1909 about the content of films: on the contrary, complaints about their vulgarity, gruesomeness and generally unedifying character are recorded as early as the 1890s, while the time-honoured practice of attributing juvenile delinquency to the cinema can be traced back to the earliest years of the present century. But it appears that the notion of film censorship, whether enshrined in law or not, was seldom mooted;[4] and when the Cinematograph Bill was introduced in Parliament early in 1909, it was put

forward as a measure solely for securing safety in premises where films
were shown. To this extent, the new Bill both formalised existing arrangements for the control of cinema, and also extended them, with limited
exemptions, to all buildings in which films were exhibited.

The Bill was inspired not just by the rapid growth of the film industry
and the ever-increasing numbers of purpose-built cinemas: at the time it
was introduced, there was also some concern about the fire danger posed
by the cinematograph. It was the latter rather than the former which
motivated a campaign by the LCC – supported by a number of other
local authorities – to secure from Parliament wider powers to regulate the
cinematograph. Even at the time, though, the risk of fire was considered
in some quarters to be overstated. Nevertheless

> The impetus of the Councils' initiative was this time too strong to stop.
> In spite of the apparent weakness of a case based on the fire danger,
> no one came forward to speak firmly against the new proposals.[5]

In such an atmosphere, after being announced in February 1909, the Cinematograph Bill enjoyed a relatively easy passage through Parliament.

Introduced initially by the Home Secretary as a private member's bill,
the new measure was promptly taken up by the Liberal government. On
its second reading in April, the Cinematograph Bill was presented by
Herbert Samuel, Under-secretary in the Home Office at the time, but in
later years twice to hold office as Home Secretary. Much was made of the
risk of fire posed by the cinematograph: the Bill, said Samuel, was intended

> to safeguard the public from the danger which arises from fires at
> cinematograph entertainments, which are especially liable to
> outbreaks of fire on account of the long highly inflammable films which
> are used in the lanterns.[6]

It was also stated that there had already been many fires, and that
control of the cinematograph was vital in order to avert the disaster which
would otherwise be virtually inevitable. An attempt by another member
to question the motives behind the Bill was brushed aside with the repeated
assertion that there had already been a considerable number of fires. At
no point either in this or in subsequent Parliamentary discussions of the
Bill are any statistics, or even actual instances, of cinematograph fires in
Britain cited. This could well be because there had in fact been no major
incidents of this kind. Nevertheless, by the time the Bill received its second
reading in the House of Lords in September, the fire hazard had become
almost mythical; after cursory debate, the measure was passed with a few
amendments and returned to the Commons in late October.[7] It received
the royal assent in November, and came into force, as the Cinematograph
Act 1909, on 1 January 1910.

In calling for the licensing of certain places of public entertainment the

new statute was in some respects an extension of the provisions of the
Disorderly Houses Act. Now, however, the public places subject to regulation were defined in technological terms:

> An exhibition of pictures or other optical effects by means of a
> cinematograph, or other similar apparatus, for the purposes of which
> inflammable films are used.[8]

This reference to inflammable films – the nitrate stock in use until the late
1940s for nearly all commercial films – is the Act's only specific concession
to the safety aspect which had so dominated discussions of the measure
both within and outside Parliament. Details of safety provisions were to
be dealt with in regulations issued separately by the Home Office, and
these were to be incorporated in the terms and conditions under which
cinematograph licences would be issued.

The county councils were to be responsible for issuing cinematograph
licences (Section 2(1)), but were entitled to delegate these powers to other
specified bodies (Section 5). Licensing authorities were also empowered to
determine the conditions under which licences were granted – a provision
which was to prove crucial *vis-à-vis* film censorship. The first Home Office
regulations under the Act, published in December 1909, were concerned
exclusively with the safety of cinema buildings: the number and location
of exits, the enclosure of the projector, the encasement of films, the type of
lighting used, the placement of fire appliances, and so on. But local
licensing authorities were quick to take advantage of the latitude the Act
appeared to offer in the matter of determining licensing conditions. Even
before the statute came into force, the LCC had recommended a condition
prohibiting exhibitions of films on Sundays.[9] The Cinematograph Act was
already being used for a purpose other than that which had supposedly
inspired it.

The imposition of a 'six-day licence' condition forbidding Sunday film
shows soon became widespread. The film trade, which had originally
supported the new legislation, began to complain about the way it was
being enforced. Over the next fifteen years or so, the trade involved itself
in a series of attempts to enlist the support of statute law in protecting its
own interests against the regulative activities of local cinema licensing
authorities. First to be subjected to challenge in the courts was the power
of local authorities to impose licensing conditions unrelated to safety. In
the first major test case brought under the Cinematograph Act, an exhibitor
had successfully argued in a magistrates' court that a ban on film shows
on Sundays, Good Friday and Christmas Day was *ultra vires* (exceeded the
powers enshrined in) the Act. The licensing authority concerned – the LCC
– appealed against this decision, and judgment in the High Court went in
favour of the Council on the grounds that Section 2(1) of the Act (which
stated that 'A county council may grant licences . . . on such terms and

under such restrictions as . . . the council may by the respective licences determine') did in fact give local licensing authorities power to impose licensing conditions which were not strictly relevant to safety. In the decision in this case, the relevant section of the Act was held 'to confer on the county council a discretion as to the conditions they will impose, so long as these conditions are not unreasonable.'[10]

Although this judgment seemed to make it possible for local authorities to place a variety of non-safety conditions on cinematograph licences, some of these were subsequently challenged at law on the grounds that they were 'unreasonable'. For example, a 1915 judgment determined that a condition requiring the exclusion of children under fourteen from a cinema after 9p.m. was in fact unreasonable and *ultra vires*.[11] This judgment, however, is exceptional: in the majority of cases of this kind brought before the courts, the discretion of local authorities to determine licensing conditions was upheld. By the mid-1910s, in consequence, it was widely accepted that licensing conditions could legitimately deal, among other things, with the contents of films shown on licensed premises.

The film industry ultimately failed, therefore, to obtain legal backing for its efforts to set limits upon local cinema licensing authorities' implementation of the Cinematograph Act. In this atmosphere, the extension of these powers to films and their content was effected virtually without protest. The 1909 Act, supposedly not intended as a measure for dealing with the contents of films, eventually opened a legal path to certain practices of film censorship. Within a year or two of the Act's passage, a few authorities had already begun to include as a condition of licence a rule to the effect that publicly exhibited films should not be immoral or indecent in character. Over the next few years, this practice was to become much more widespread.

Films which might have been considered improper could, of course, equally have fallen within the broader purview of statutory provisions on indecency and obscenity. Films were also subject to sanction under common law, the relevant offences being outraging public decency, conspiracy to outrage public decency, and obscene libel. The existence of such legal sanctions notwithstanding, it was unheard-of at this period for films shown in public cinemas to be prosecuted for indecency or obscenity. The practices of film censorship which grew out of the Cinematograph Act effected much more stringent controls over the contents of films than any legislation directed specifically at indecent or obscene publications could possibly have done. Besides which, unlike indecency and obscenity laws, these practices operated in an *a priori* manner, in that regulation was exercised before films were exhibited, not afterwards.[12]

As far as the content of films was concerned, then, the cinema licensing system remained the principal instrument of legal regulation. But full legal confirmation of the view that local licensing authorities could assume powers of film censorship under the Cinematograph Act's provisions for cinema licensing did not come about until the 1920s, with judgments in two further cases involving disputes between film exhibitors and local licensing authorities. The effect of these judgments was to clarify the limits of local authority powers of censorship *vis-à-vis* those of the British Board of Film Censors.

In *Ellis* v. *Dubowski* (1921), it was held unreasonable and *ultra vires* the Cinematograph Act for a licensing authority to impose a condition prohibiting the exhibition of films which had not been passed by the BBFC. The grounds for this judgment were that such a condition transferred a power which belonged in law to the licensing authority – namely the power to censor films – to an organisation with no statutory or constitutional authority (the BBFC was a voluntary body without legal or official status). The judge, however, did suggest that

if the condition had reserved to the [licensing authority] the right to review the decisions of the Board, the condition would have been reasonable and *intra vires*.[13]

In other words, a condition endorsing the BBFC's decisions on films might have been legally acceptable had it been clear that the Board's decision was not being substituted for that of the licensing authority. The powers of the latter in this area were not, significantly, in dispute.

Any remaining uncertainty on this score was settled in the courts some four years later, when the LCC sought to test the legality of one of its licensing conditions. This provided that

no film . . . which has not been passed for universal exhibition by the British Board of Film Censors shall be exhibited in the premises without the express consent of the Council during the time that any child under . . . the age of 16 years is therein. . . .

The suggestion put forward in *Ellis* v. *Dubowski* was taken up in the judgment in this case. The LCC's condition was held to be legal because in reserving to itself the right to review the BBFC's decisions, the LCC did not relinquish any of its powers under the Cinematograph Act. In his summing up, Lord Hewart reminded the court that 'under the Cinematograph Act, 1909, the licensing authority is given, and no doubt most deliberately given, very wide powers'.[14] If there were any lingering doubts that these powers included film censorship, they were dispelled by this judgment, and the question was never again to be raised in the courts. The censorship of films in Britain consequently acquired a foundation in law without ever figuring centrally in any statute or case.

This being so, how – legally speaking – was it organised and administered? The government department responsible for implementing the Cinematograph Act was the Home Office, and the Act provided for safety regulations to be issued by the Home Secretary. The Act, as I have noted, was enforced 'on the ground' through a system of licensing of cinema buildings, administered by county councils or their specified delegates. The Home Office regulations, which were to be incorporated in local authorities' conditions for granting licences, were issued in the form of delegated legislation – statutory instruments which, though not actually appearing in statute, carry the status and force of law. Statutory instruments issued under the Cinematograph Act related exclusively to technical aspects of safety, such as fire precautions, lighting, and standards for electrical installations.

But if censorship was not touched upon either in statute law or in delegated legislation, the Home Office assumed a good deal of 'advisory' responsibility for the powers of censorship assumed by local authorities. On this issue, the Home Office communicated directly with licensing authorities by means of administrative circulars, documents which do not in fact carry the status of legislation.[15] These contained advice to local licensing authorities about their powers under the Cinematograph Act and offered them encouragement and guidance in using these powers. Censorship matters were dealt with exclusively through administrative circulars, and the earliest communication of this kind was sent to licensing authorities in May 1916. Circulars were the means by which the Home Office conveyed to local licensing authorities its recommendations for cinema licensing conditions, specifically for conditions relating to the content of films.

Twice during the period covered by this inquiry – in 1917 and in 1923 – the Home Office issued model licensing conditions in circular form. These included rules prohibiting the exhibition of films and the display of advertisements 'likely to be injurious to public morality, or to encourage or incite to crime, or to lead to disorder . . .', and a provision that films could be examined by the licensing authority before being exhibited.[16] The objective of these and other Home Office circulars was to persuade local authorities to make full use of their censorship powers, and ultimately to bring about national uniformity in film censorship practices.

Thus, although in law local licensing authorities were the bodies responsible for film censorship (and as such were the targets of legal action on this and other matters relating to cinema licensing), the Home Office – which, strictly speaking, had no legal standing in this area – did seek to influence events. Indeed, one commentator has noted the 'deference' with which a Home Office circular would be received by most local authorities.[17] The administration, in short, sought to engineer consent to certain practices of film censorship on the part of agencies with legal powers in this area. This situation holds obvious potential for conflict.

The conflict potential was realised when the Home Office tried to bring about across-the-board uniformity in censorship practices. Since coercion was out of the question, if the Home Office wanted uniformity its only recourse was persuasion. And yet – since its role was meant to be merely advisory – even the gentlest cajolery could scarcely be tendered publicly, while the desired outcome could by no means be guaranteed. Some local authorities were very keen to maintain their independence from central government, in film censorship as in other matters. In these circumstances, relations between the Home Office and such independently-inclined and influential cinema licensing authorities as the London County Council were sometimes rather strained. The opposing pulls of national uniformity and local autonomy are evident in at least one of the case histories in this book.

At the same time, the law itself – despite its implicit endorsement of a certain machinery of film censorship – rarely involved itself openly in such matters. So, for instance, when the film industry sought legal support for its resistance to the powers of local authorities, it rapidly became apparent that such support would not be easily come by. In any case, after the late 1910s direct resort to law was rare, and *Mills* v. *LCC* in 1925 was the last time a test case under the Cinematograph Act went to the High Court. The principal 'official' institutional protagonists in matters of film censorship were thus the local licensing authorities on one side and the Home Office on the other, with the law itself taking a back seat. Censorship, while founded in law, nevertheless contrived to avoid being pinned down by it; and another – and in many respects the most prominent – censorship institution entered the arena with no legal backing at all. This fourth contender is the British Board of Film Censors.

The British Board of Film Censors and 'voluntary' censorship

During the two or three years after the Cinematograph Act was passed, some uncertainty about local authorities' discretion in attaching non-safety regulations to cinema licences prevailed. But if it was nonetheless taken for granted that they could assume powers of censorship under the cinema licensing system, few authorities were at first inclined or equipped to do so. Unless an authority had the resources to pre-censor films exhibited in cinemas in its area, any condition concerning their content could only be enforced after the fact, either by prosecution or, more usually in cases of infringement, by threats to withdraw the licences of offending cinemas. Consequently, censorship was uneven throughout the country, and in some areas virtually non-existent. By the end of 1911, cinema was attracting a good deal of opprobrium, and existing forms of regulation were widely denounced as inadequate and ineffective. A formal system of film censorship was seriously proposed for the first time, and the film industry, which had hitherto regarded all forms of censorship as an undesirable restriction on trade, now began to fear government intervention.[18]

At this point, accepting that censorship in some form or other was probably inevitable, and with a view to averting what it saw as the worst possible option – state censorship – the industry sought Home Office approval for a trade-sponsored scheme. In February 1912, the Home Secretary received a deputation of film manufacturers and renters, who submitted the proposals for a Board of Film Censors to be set up under the aegis of the film industry.[19] The trade's initiative was not at this point actively discouraged, but some months were to elapse before the scheme received more positive, if still informal, support from the Home Office. Early in November, G. A. Redford was appointed president of what was now called the British Board of Film Censors. Redford, having been Examiner of Plays in the Lord Chamberlain's office, had prior knowledge and experience of censorship, if not of cinema.

The appointment of a man with such a background was undoubtedly made with the objective of convincing the Home Office of the new Board's serious intent and independence from trade influence. A few days afterwards, the sponsors of the scheme met once more with the Home Secretary, this time offering a detailed plan for the organisation and operation of the Board of Censors, a body which, they argued, would provide 'an absolutely independent censorship, which it is felt is essential to meet the present objections by certain Licensing Authorities'. The Board would be financed by a set fee per foot of film viewed, and the financial side of the operation would be the responsibility of the Incorporated Association of Kinematograph Manufacturers – this being a move to forestall allegations of producer or exhibitor interference in the Board's decisions. The two-certificate system – 'U' (for universal exhibition) and 'A' (for public exhibition, i.e., for adult audiences) – was also proposed at this meeting. This system was to remain in force for many years:

> The object of these two certificates is to meet, as far as possible, the complaints that have been made by licensing authorities in respect of the non-suitability of certain films for children's entertainments.[20]

If this move towards self-regulation on the part of the film trade was made with a view to averting government intervention, it was certainly, for a time at least, successful. The British Board of Film Censors began its active work on the first day of 1913, announcing that 'No film subject will be passed that is not clean and wholesome, and absolutely above suspicion'. In the Board's first annual report, it is stated that of 7510 films submitted in 1913, 6861 had been passed 'U', 627 passed 'A', and 22 entirely rejected. The grounds given for exception and rejection include indelicate sexual situations, the ridiculing of religion, excessive gruesomeness and cruelty, procuration and abduction, and 'native customs in foreign lands abhorrent to British ideas'.[21]

But such vigilance failed to satisfy the critics. One of the problems the

Board had to face was that, as a voluntary organisation, its decisions were advisory rather than mandatory, so licensing authorities could accept or reject them as they chose. The effectiveness of the BBFC depended upon the support of local authorities, and this was not immediately forthcoming. By the end of 1914, twenty-four authorities had announced that they would accept the Board's rulings on films, and in the following year twelve more gave such an undertaking. Given that licensing authorities in the UK numbered upwards of five hundred at this time, the voluntary system of film censorship was obviously making slow headway. Moreover, even before the end of the BBFC's first year in operation, renewed demands for official government censorship were being made. These were resisted at first by the Home Office, on the grounds mainly that any change of this kind would require new legislation; this would give rise to 'public discussion and controversy', always officially regarded as highly undesirable. However, many local authorities, and indeed the Home Office itself, considered that the BBFC's standards were not tough enough. This made demands for state censorship all the harder to resist, though resist them the Home Office continued for a while to do.[22]

But 1916 saw a shift in Home Office policy on film censorship. Herbert Samuel, prime mover of the 1909 Act and now newly appointed Home Secretary, took a keener interest than his predecessor in the censorship question, and was more favourably disposed to the idea of an official scheme. In May a circular letter was sent out informing local licensing authorities that in view of the inadequacy of existing controls on film content, new censorship provisions were under consideration. These would take the form of 'An official and independent censorship . . . established by the government'.[23] The reactions of licensing authorities to this proposal were being solicited because the Home Office had decided to introduce the new scheme 'by administrative action' – in other words, not to bring in fresh legislation. For this to come about, local authorities would have to relinquish their existing legal powers voluntarily. The vast majority of them seemed quite prepared to do this.

The film trade, already disgruntled at the way the Cinematograph Act was being enforced, disheartened by the failure of the courts to curb licensing authorities' powers, and anxious to keep the Board of Censors in operation,[24] was disturbed at this new development. Soon after the local authorities had been circularised on the question of official censorship, the exhibitors' association met with the Home Secretary and suggested that if government censorship were to be introduced, it ought to be done openly by legislation, and not covertly through the administrative process. Nevertheless, the Home Office proceeded with its existing proposals, and in October 1916 the Cabinet was alerted that an official film censorship scheme would come into operation early in the following year.[25] By this time, however, the trade had already moved into action with a campaign against the government's plans. In November George Redford died and, in a bid to enhance the BBFC's credibility with the Home Office, was replaced as the Board's president by T. P. O'Connor, an MP and journalist and also a past president of the Cinematograph Exhibitors' Association.

Despite these manoeuvrings, Samuel's scheme for state censorship might still have gone through in the new year had it not been for a change of government at the end of 1916. The new Home Secretary decided to drop the idea, explaining to local authorities that in view of the trade's opposition, it was 'impracticable now to proceed with the proposal, and . . . the question of a central censorship must be postponed, until there is opportunity for legislation'. In the event, no such opportunity arose. Meanwhile, though, the Home Office proposed encouraging local licensing authorities to make more effective use of their powers of censorship under the Cinematograph Act. With this objective, the first set of Home Office model conditions for cinema licences was sent out with the circular: these were aimed at 'checking the exhibition of objectionable films'.[26] At this point, however, the Home Office made no mention of the BBFC. In fact, overt government support for the Board was not to be forthcoming for some years: it was only in 1923 that the Home Office, in a revised set of model conditions, recommended that licensing authorities should, as a matter of policy, follow the Board's advice on films.

The six years between the government's decision to shelve the state censorship scheme and its eventual endorsement of the Board of Censors mark a period of intense struggle between the Board, the local licensing authorities and the Home Office itself around powers of, and responsibilities for, film censorship. Difficulties arose when many local licensing authorities failed to heed the BBFC's recommendations regarding the certification and censorship of individual films. This, together with local variations in censorship practices, was regarded by the Home Office as highly trouble-some. The Home Office deprecated the situation because complaints about particular films and their apparently hit-and-miss regulation were repeat-edly being directed at government. The film trade complained that arbi-trary and inconsistent local censorship decisions were ruinous for business. And the BBFC itself was all the while anxious to enhance its authority and credibility. All of the films discussed in the case histories were in one way or another caught up in the struggles of these years.

During much of this time, the BBFC and its lack of authority were regarded – by the Home Office, at least – as the root cause of all the trouble provoked by exhibitions of allegedly 'objectionable' films. If national uniformity in film censorship was to be brought about without government intervention, the Board's decisions would have to carry sufficient weight on their own merits to persuade licensing authorities to accept them. The fate of the Board of Censors hung in the balance, then, for the option of government censorship was by no means decisively rejected in 1917: it was still considered a serious possibility until 1921 at least. Nevertheless, the Home Office was not particularly eager to reopen the question, for it was sensitive to the fact that the work of an official censorship body would be open to public scrutiny and therefore potentially 'embarrassing . . . to the minister responsible for it'.[27]

At the same time, though, the 1917 circular had still not produced a great deal of uniformity between licensing authorities. Furthermore, the alternative route to uniformity – widespread acceptance by licensing authorities of the BBFC's advice on films – seemed at this point equally out of reach: a questionnaire sent to local authorities in 1919 elicited the information that only twenty counties and county boroughs stipulated in their licensing conditions that all films exhibited should have a BBFC certificate.[28] If a state take-over of film censorship was to be avoided, the work of the Board of Censors would have to command much wider local backing; but this was likely to be achieved only if the Home Office could shed its reluctance to support the Board. The BBFC did eventually get government backing, though in a characteristically roundabout way: the lead in the matter was taken not by the Home Office, but by two important licensing authorities.

In August 1920, the Middlesex County Council resolved to include in its cinema licensing conditions the rule that 'no film be shown which has not been certified for public exhibition by the British Board of Film Censors'. The legality of this clause was to be at issue when *Ellis* v. *Dubowski* came to the courts in the following July. A cinema in Twickenham had infringed the ruling by exhibiting *Auction of Souls*, which – as a result of the BBFC's policy on 'propaganda' films (see chapter 4) – had no censor's certificate.[29] The proprietor of the cinema was taken to court under Section 3 of the Cinematograph Act, in what was in effect a legal test of the MCC's new condition.

In this instance, the action of the cinema proprietor in screening an uncertificated film constituted a gesture of resistance not only to the powers of a local licensing authority, but also to the BBFC. Space for this sort of action existed in a situation in which the Board's powers *vis-à-vis* local authorities remained uncertain. As noted earlier in this chapter, the judgment in this case made it clear – if it had not been so already – that the activities of the Board of Censors could enjoy no privileged legal status, and that the final arbiter in matters of film censorship had to be the local cinema licensing authority. At the same time, the judgment also suggested a resolution of the regulative contradiction on the one hand of a censorship body offering a nationwide service but lacking legal authority; and on the other of legally-constituted censorship practices which were uneven in their operation and effects. In short, the *Ellis* v. *Dubowski* ruling hinted at a solution to the difficulties faced by the Home Office in engineering local consent to national uniformity.

More decisive in this context, however, was a move – only a few months after *Ellis* v. *Dubowski*, and partly in response to it – on the part of the London County Council. In December 1921, the LCC's Theatres and Music Halls Committee, which had consistently acted as a pacesetter for other local authorities in cinema licensing practices, issued a new set of licensing conditions. In its ruling

> That no film . . . which has not been passed for 'universal' or 'public' exhibition by the British Board of Film Censors shall be exhibited without the express consent of the Council

the Committee endorsed the work of the BBFC by adopting the suggestion offered in the *Ellis* v. *Dubowski* judgment. The new conditions also required that cinema proprietors observe the recommendations as to suitable audiences embodied in the BBFC's 'U' and 'A' certificates, and that the Board's certificate be displayed on the screen before each exhibition of a film. Before taking this step, the LCC had privately consulted with, and obtained the support of, the Home Office, which saw the adoption of these conditions by a leading local authority as a means of protecting the BBFC (and itself, no doubt) against demands for state censorship.[30]

Once made public, the new LCC conditions roused fury among exhibitors, who were particularly incensed by the attempt to make the 'A' certificate mandatory by excluding under-16s from 'A' films. When the trade made representations to the Council, and ultimately threatened to make this an issue in the forthcoming local elections, the LCC backed down to the extent of adding a rider that the condition would only apply to children unaccompanied by parents or guardians, and agreeing to postpone implementation of the reformulated condition (which did not actually come into force until January 1923). Meanwhile, the Home Office decided to wait until controversy died down before recommending that other local authorities adopt the LCC's conditions. It was rumoured, too, that the LCC was preparing to test the 'A' films condition by taking legal action against an exhibitor infringing it.[31]

In May 1923, a few months after the delayed implementation of the disputed condition, the Home Office called a conference of representatives of local licensing authorities, with a view to assessing the extent to which the LCC's new rules would be acceptable elsewhere in the country. Although some authorities had still to be convinced of the merits of the BBFC, and while doubts were expressed about the enforceability of the 'A' films condition, the majority of those present favoured the idea of a new set of model conditions based on the LCC's precedent.[32] This would meet both of the Home Office's objectives at a stroke: if the LCC's conditions were widely adopted, then the BBFC would have obtained the general endorsement it needed, while at the same time a greater uniformity between localities in censorship practices would also be assured. Besides which, should such a scheme prove effective, it would offer a convincing reply to those still clamouring for the introduction of state censorship of films. These moves resulted in the formulation of a new set of Home Office model conditions, which were circulated to local authorities in July 1923. By contrast with the 1917 circular, the BBFC is not only mentioned, but its work is also praised as having achieved 'considerable success'. The conditions themselves are the same as those recommended in 1917, with the addition of three new clauses based upon the LCC's new rulings.[33]

The new circular was followed up in the spring of 1924 by a survey designed to gauge the extent to which the revised conditions were being taken up. The results, according to the Home Office, showed 'fairly satisfactory progress in the direction of greater uniformity'. Within a few weeks, the LCC's long-awaited test case made its first court appearance. In a hearing involving the proprietor of a cinema in the Old Kent Road, magistrates at Lambeth Police Court ruled that the LCC was not acting unreasonably nor exceeding its powers in imposing a condition of licence stating that unaccompanied children under sixteen should be excluded from cinemas during the exhibition of BBFC-certificated 'A' films. On appeal, in *Mills* v. *London County Council* (1925), this ruling was endorsed. The new conditions – and, indirectly, the BBFC and its system of film certification – were thus given the blessing of the courts.[34] Although a few local authorities continued to take an independent line, the approach enshrined in the 1923 circular was to set the pattern for practices of film censorship throughout Britain for decades to follow. And the Home Office, now openly supporting the British Board of Film Censors and its work, adopted a policy of defending the Board against all demands for official censorship.

The events narrated in this chapter suggest that the birth of film censorship in Britain cannot be pinned down to any precise date, but rather that it was a process drawn out over a period of some fifteen years or more. At hand in this extended genesis was a whole array of discourses and powers, among them those of the institutions I have discussed here: the law, the film industry, local cinema licensing authorities, the Home Office, and the British Board of Film Censors. But the activities and the interactions of these 'censorship institutions', though of obvious significance, are neither exhaustive nor decisive in the formation of practices of censorship in the cinema. The extensiveness, complexity, fluidity and dynamism of the powers at work in film censorship are more fully revealed in the case histories which follow.

3

The Morale of the Race and the Amusement of the Public

The interests of the State are bound up not with the quantity but with the quality of its citizens.

Havelock Ellis, 1910

A Hollywood film in the USA

In April 1916, a film entitled *Where Are My Children* was released in the USA, to favourable reception by both critics and audiences. It was written and directed by Lois Weber, today regarded by some historians of cinema as 'the most important woman director of the silent era',[1] but in her own time ranked among the top few Hollywood film directors, without qualification as to gender. In 1916, Weber was leading director at Universal Studios where, exceptionally, she enjoyed complete freedom in overseeing most stages of the film-making process – choice of stories and actors, writing of scripts (which she invariably did herself), as well as direction. Lois Weber made her mark by specialising in films whose promotion stressed their high quality and moral rectitude, films which took up, within the prevailing conventions of fictional narrative cinema, burning social and moral issues of the day. Her stories were presented as serious in intent, addressing themselves to a 'thinking' audience. In the mid-1910s, the combination of lofty moral tone, topicality and controversiality with 'good stories' had – from the film industry's point of view, certainly – the additional merit of promising success at the box-office (always provided, of course, that any objections to the films' controversial subject matter could be negotiated – though at the same time these could also be played on for their publicity value).

Where Are My Children themes of birth control and abortion were highly charged issues at this period on both sides of the Atlantic. In the USA, Margaret Sanger's proselytising activities on behalf of contraception and her ensuing brushes with the law had served to bring these matters to the very forefront of public consciousness.[2] But if the contentiousness of the subject matter of Lois Weber's film elicited rumblings of censorship, it was nevertheless possible for *Where Are My Children* to be successful both critically and financially, in the USA. It was a different story in Britain,

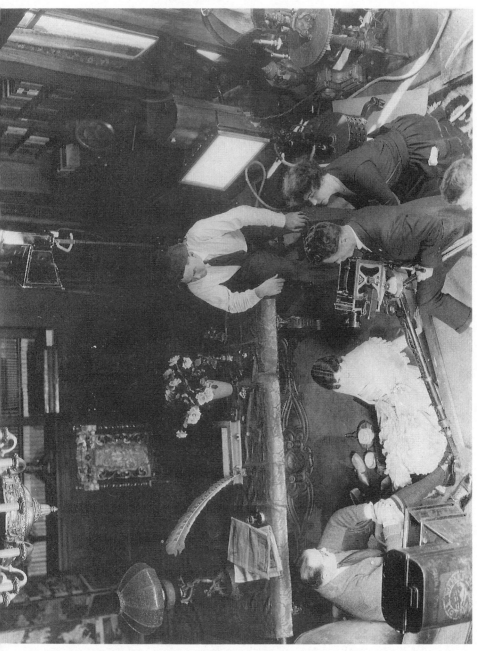

Fig. 1 Lois Weber
(bottom right)
directing a film

where the film was in effect suppressed for a variety of reasons, not all of them having directly to do either with censorship or indeed with the film's content. On its arrival in Britain, *Where Are My Children* became caught up in – and its suppression participated in the production of – a series of distinctions which were to sustain certain constructions of cinema as a public sphere. These constructions in turn would frame the discursive practices and power relations governing the regulation of cinema in Britain.

Where Are My Children deals with birth control and abortion. The film's hero, Richard Walton, is a district attorney with a keen interest in eugenics and a great desire to have children of his own: his childlessness, unbeknown to him, is due to his frivolous wife's patronage of an abortionist, Dr Malfit. Walton is prosecutor in the trial of one Dr Homer, who is charged with disseminating 'indecent' literature – a book about birth control – but his assistance in the man's conviction goes against his own inclinations. The Waltons' housekeeper brings her young daughter to stay in the house; the innocent girl is soon seduced by Mrs Walton's rakish brother. She becomes pregnant, and with Mrs Walton's reluctant collusion is sent to Malfit, who botches the operation. The girl dies, and the abortionist is brought to justice. Walton secures his conviction, and the guilty man is sentenced to fifteen years' hard labour. As he is led away, Malfit accuses his prosecutor of hypocrisy, and this leads Walton to the discovery that his wife has had several abortions. Returning home, he accuses her of murdering his unborn children. Repentant, Mrs Walton tries to conceive, but without success. The couple grow old together, childless and lonely.

However discreetly treated, this, in 1916, was highly censorable material, a fact of which the film's producers, Universal, were evidently well aware: release, they claimed, was delayed for a while because of possible censorship problems.[3] These did not materialise, however – or at least not immediately. On its eventual release in early April, *Where Are My Children* enjoyed an extended, uninterrupted and highly successful run at a Broadway cinema, and was later shown in other movie theatres in Manhattan.[4] It was well received, too, by the critics, who praised the film's delicate handling of sensitive subject matter, its attention to significant detail, and its powerful dramatic qualities: the forecast was clearly for success.[5]

Nevertheless, the risk of censorship remained. Only a year earlier, in *Mutual Film Corporation* v. *Industrial Commission of Ohio*, the US Supreme Court had ruled that films were not entitled to protection as 'speech' under the First Amendment to the Constitution, on the grounds that cinema was 'business, pure and simple'.[6] This decision opened the way for a variety of practices of prior censorship, all of them, until the *Mutual* decision was revoked in 1952, perfectly legitimate. Self-regulation by the film trade did not come fully into operation until the 1930s: until that time film censorship rested largely, in areas which had such bodies, with state and local boards of censors. These arrangements produced a good deal of unevenness in rules and standards of censorship between localities. But at the same time a producer whose film was cut or banned in one area might still be in a position to market it elsewhere in the USA. Something of this sort appears to have happened in the case of *Where Are My Children*.

Where censor boards did not exist or were inactive, however, various forms of censorship could still be deployed. For example, in some areas exhibitors could have their trading licenses revoked if they screened 'objectionable' films. It was this possibility, more than that of prior censorship, that Universal probably had in mind in deciding to delay the New York release of *Where Are My Children*: that the local license commissioner might place a ban on the film on grounds that it dealt with a controversial topic.[7] As it turned out, in fact, the New York City commissioner did not move against the film: in nearby Brooklyn, though, it was subjected to restraint, but through the courts rather than through licensing regulations.

In June, the president of the Universal Film Exchange – the film's distributor – and the manager of the Rialto Theatre, Brooklyn were summonsed in response to a complaint that *Where Are My Children* was unfit for exhibition. The manager of another Brooklyn cinema which was showing the film was also brought before a magistrate, but in the latter instance the complaint was dismissed. Trade journal reports of these cases argued that pre-censorship was unnecessary because 'moving picture offenders can be reached by law whenever those offended wish to act'.[8] This was an attack not only on the *Mutual* decision's support for the prior censorship of films, but also on a bill being discussed at the time in Congress, one of a series of attempts made at this period to bring in a federal system of film censorship. No federal film censorship bill was ever passed, but repeated efforts in this direction over a number of years served to keep the film industry constantly aware of the damage to business which could ensue if certain marks were overstepped.[9]

The Brooklyn District Attorney, these reports imply, was engaged on a personal mission to stamp out 'pictures that deal with sex problems'. That film censorship in the USA at this period was erratic enough to accommodate extremes of activity and inactivity, from the crusading zeal of morally outraged officials to the *laissez-faire* attitude of many a local bureaucracy, is evident in the further vicissitudes of *Where Are My Children*. In Boston, for example – where the film opened in July to packed houses – the local censorship commission, considered one of the most rigid in the country, said it would not interfere with the film unless a complaint were received.[10] At the other extreme, the film was rejected several times by censors in Pennsylvania, and on final appeal in October was described by that state's Chief Censor as 'unspeakably vile. . . . It is a mess of filth, and no revision, however drastic, could ever help it any. It is not fit for decent people to see'. Nevertheless, those wishing to judge the merits of *Where Are My Children* for themselves had only to cross the state line and travel to Atlantic City, 'where the film is enjoying an immense popularity'[11] – enhanced, no doubt, by the well-publicised denunciations of the Pennsylvania censors.

Despite – or indeed perhaps because of – its outrageous subject matter and consequent susceptibility to censorship, *Where Are My Children* apparently did very well in the USA: according to one film historian, it 'rocketed Weber's name to larger audiences, bigger box-office returns, and an even higher annual income'.[12] This could have been possible only in a situation in which film censorship – its practice and its effectivity – was overall rather uneven and haphazard. If the producers were worried that the film might be censored, they were in no position to predict with any degree of certainty whether or not it actually would be. And once a film was made, there was often little to lose and much to gain by releasing it, particularly if, as in this case, it could be promoted as yet another quality product from the workshop of Lois Weber.

Even at this relatively early period in the history of cinema, a film's promotion in terms of its authorship could sometimes help to ensure its success, as well as protect it from interference at the hands of the censors. While in later years the label 'art' attached to a film would often serve to shield it from the full rigours of censorship, in the mid-1910s it seems that a reputation for providing quality in the form of moral rectitude such as that enjoyed by a director of the calibre of Lois Weber had much the same effect. The lofty intent informing subject matter which might otherwise be regarded as unacceptable becomes a crucial factor in the American reception of a film like *Where Are My Children*. Many would-be censors were undoubtedly disarmed by the film's own claims to be on the side of the guardians of morality. The notion that, as one reviewer hinted, its moral message tries to run with the hare and hunt with the hounds ('from the standpoint of an argument for or against birth control – it is both. It starts off seemingly as an argument in favour of birth control and suddenly switches to an argument against abortion')[13] would suggest a degree of openness which could only strengthen the film's capacity to find supporters in a variety of camps.

But in 1916 a moral message of such openness was by no means sufficient on its own to secure a film's success. This was a moment in which certain methods of cinematic narration had gained ascendancy in American cinema, and when the hegemony of the fiction feature in commercial cinema was already assured:[14] a film, in order to be successful, needed a 'good story' – a story, that is, deploying certain conventions of theme, style and narration. In some senses, certainly as far as the American market was concerned, *Where Are My Children* offered itself as at least as 'good' a story as it was a sermon.

Where Are My Children: Sermon or melodrama?

In the expository intertitle with which *Where Are My Children* begins,[15] the film proffers earnest of its own moral intent, and solicits the assent of 'intelligent people' to such a self-presentation:

> The question of birth control is now being generally discussed. All intelligent people know that birth control is a subject of serious public interest. Newspapers, magazines and books have treated different phases of this question. Can a subject thus dealt with on the printed page be denied careful dramatisation on the motion picture screen? The Universal Film Mfg Company believes not. . . .

At the same time, this rhetorical flourish addresses the audience – *au fait* with current debates in the quality print media – as itself both serious-minded and intelligent.

Where Are My Children announces right away that it is 'about' birth control, but this can be true only insofar as such a substantive concern may be articulated through the conventions of fictional narrative cinema. For *Where Are My Children* is above all a story, a fiction whose trajectory is governed by the actions and motivations of its characters. In particular, in the character of Richard Walton, the district attorney hero, the story's concern with birth control is in effect transformed into a set of personality traits and – especially – desires. In the setting in which he is most powerful – the courtroom – Walton is introduced early in the film as 'a great believer in eugenics' whose wife is 'childless'. Meanwhile, at the Waltons' large and well-appointed home, Mrs Walton reclines on a *chaise longue* eating chocolates and playing with pet dogs. Walton returns home and greets his 'childless' wife affectionately, for, 'Never dreaming it was her fault, her husband concealed his disappointment'. Walton's childlessness, then, is involuntary, and it is in fact his thwarted desire to be a father which largely governs the subsequent progress of the narrative. His interest in eugenics is a device which motivates the trial of the birth control activist Dr Homer, and adds a medico-moral gloss to Mrs Walton's 'evasion' of motherhood.

Eugenics, as a set of ideas about the physical and intellectual quality of the population and its capacity for improvement through human intervention in the form of science and/or social reform, enjoyed a great vogue in the early years of this century, fuelled by concerns about the state of what was universally termed 'the race' (at this period 'the word "race" appears to have been interchangeable with "nation", "community" or even "people" ').[16] Eugenics offered the prospect of reversing what was perceived to be a deterioration in the quality of the population. The lower classes, the 'feeble-minded', and the 'degenerate' were breeding, it was feared, at a rate which threatened the extinction of the 'best' elements of the race (namely, the middle classes), amongst whom the birth rate appeared to be in sharp decline.

The eugenic theme of *Where Are My Children* explains the apparent inconsistency of the film's pro-birth control and anti-abortion stances. During the trial of Dr Homer, the defendant's work among the poor is portrayed in three flashback-style sequences which punctuate the court-room scene in which he is being cross-examined by Walton. The first shows a room in a slum household and a young mother of three infant children who is obviously ill, probably suffering from TB or syphilis. As the doctor enters and examines the smallest baby, the mother stands by, coughing and sobbing. In the brief second flashback, Dr Homer stands on a bridge, looking over the parapet. He calls a policeman, possibly having witnessed a suicide, though this is not made explicit. The third sequence shows a working-class couple, their children present in the room, in the throes of a violent argument. The woman throws a pan at the man and they start fighting. The doctor arrives on the street, enters the house, and attempts to separate the couple, but is ejected by both of them. Back in the courtroom, the doctor says: 'These conditions prove to me the necessity of world-wide enlightenment on the subject of birth control', though what the flashbacks actually suggest is that it is not the whole world but the poor and the lower classes who stand in need of such enlightenment. For it is they who – as a cut-in close shot of an excerpt from Homer's book states – are 'ignorant and undisciplined', allowing 'unwanted children [to] be born to suffer blind-ness, disease or insanity'. Dr Homer is not an advocate so much of choice in matters of fertility, then, as of negative eugenics, the discouragement of breeding by the 'unfit'. So, it seems, is Richard Walton, who regards some of the delinquents he deals with in the course of his work as 'ill-born'. 'If the mystery of birth were understood', he says, 'crime would be wiped out.'

Evidently, the bourgeois Mrs Walton's strategies of family limitation do not fall into the same category as those advocated by Dr Homer and her husband – for these apply only to certain sections of the population, namely, the 'unfit': positive eugenics demands that the fertility of the 'best stocks' be encouraged. The scene of Dr Homer's trial is cross-cut with sequences showing Mrs Walton with her frivolous 'social butterfly' women friends. While the doctor is being brought to book for his efforts at improving the race, Mrs Walton unconcernedly procures an abortion for one of her associates. Walton, downcast by the trial's outcome, returns to an empty house, and while waiting for his wife to come home, gazes with longing at the three young children of the eugenically-disposed family next door. It is at this moment that the narrative's two main trajectories intersect. If the lack constructed in the world of the fiction – Mrs Walton's of children – could be set to rights by her assuming what is termed in the film 'the diadem of motherhood', not only would the hero's desire for a family be satisfied, so too would the demands of a positive eugenics.

These would hold that, for a woman of the 'best type', motherhood is not merely the true fulfilment of her sex, but also her responsibility – as 'Nature's supreme organ of the future' – to the race. For such a woman to 'evade' motherhood by resorting to abortion or other forms of birth control was thus doubly reprehensible.[17] The eugenic theme, then, readily accommodates what the *Variety* reviewer saw as a contradictory stance on birth control. For what is at issue is not so much birth control *per se* as the quality of the population and the control of fertility, in one direction or another, so as to enhance it. However, once it is established that in undergoing abortions Mrs Walton is shirking her duty to the race, the narrative can confine itself more closely to the domains of individual psychology, frustrated desire and melodrama, with which the Hollywood feature film was, already in the mid-1910s, much more at home.

Not only is Mrs Walton denying her husband's dearest wish, she is doing so deceitfully, while also, presumably, having sex 'for its own sake'. In terms of the discourse on femininity constructed by the film, this amounts to nothing less than an unnatural corruption of the proper balance of power in the domestic sphere. The conventions of the moral tale demand that such duplicity be discovered, and punished. This comes about by means of a subplot whose narrative function is, in the final instance, to expose to Walton – *qua* DA – the activities of the abortionist, Dr Malfit, and in consequence to bring home to Walton – *qua* husband – the realisation that his wife has all along been making use of the abortionist's services. But along the way the subplot does considerably more than this, constructing certain discourses around femininity, innocence and corruption, discourses which implicate the film further within a particular set of conventions of cinematic narrativity.

Mrs Walton's reprobate brother arrives at the Waltons' for what turns out to be an extended stay. On the same day, the Waltons' housekeeper brings her daughter, who has just left school, to live in the house until a job can be found for her. The girl, with her frilly smock and long, beribboned hair loose about her shoulders, is the very epitome of the naive *ingénue* of silent cinema. Eyed lasciviously by the brother, she responds by shyly averting her face from his gaze. Eventually, however, the inevitable happens ('Practice teaches men of this class the bold methods that sweep inexperienced girls off their feet'): she is seduced and becomes pregnant.

It was the old, old tragedy, and one of the 'unwanted ones' was called to earth.

All the outward marks of sexual innocence now relinquished – she wears a dark tailored dress and has her hair in a bun – the girl seeks out the brother in the garden to tell him of her plight. He abruptly pushes her away and runs indoors to his sister, who has by this time seen the error of her ways and decided 'to conquer her selfishness and prepare for motherhood'. She is nevertheless persuaded, albeit reluctantly, to give her brother the address of Dr Malfit for a 'friend . . . in trouble'. This turns out to be Mrs Walton's undoing. But this substantial subplot effects more than simply the exposure and punishment of one character.

The lengthy scenes involving the brother and the housekeeper's daughter before the girl's seduction are significant in that, for a film made as early as 1916, they contain some rather elaborate point-of-view and shot/reverse shot figures.[18] These foreshadow the centrality of the look in the cinematic image as signifying certain relations of gender and sexuality. For example, the scene, already noted, in which the pair first meet contains a sustained shot/reverse shot sequence which affirms the man's sexual predatoriness, as the instigator of the look, and the sexual innocence of the girl as its reluctant recipient:

1 CU brother, eyeing the girl obliquely
2 Reverse shot of 1 – the girl looks up shyly
3 As shot 1 – the man continues looking
4 As shot 2 – the girl turns away.

Later, the brother is twice shown following the girl, spying on her as – in an iconographic gesture equating nature with innocence – she gathers flowers in the garden. He sidles out of his hiding place, approaches her, speaks, and kisses her. From this moment on, her innocence lost, the girl is never again to be constructed as object of the gaze – of her seducer, of any other character in the fiction, or indeed of the film's spectator.

This, given the association between looking and sexual pleasure – specifically in their cinematic organisation through certain conventions of iconography, shot scale and editing –[19] betokens an eroticisation of female sexual innocence. An obsession with female sexual purity is a defining characteristic of silent cinema, though it is difficult to judge how common it would have been in 1916 for such innocence to be constructed through the particular organisation of cinematic point-of-view deployed in *Where Are My Children*. Whatever the case, sequences involving point-of-view assume particular significance in this film, if only because there are rather few of them. The housekeeper's daughter is, for a time, the object of the look of Mrs Walton's sexually predatory brother. But the look of the film's hero, Richard Walton himself, also motivates point-of-view shots on at least two occasions: as he watches children playing in the garden of the house next door, and as he admires his sister's baby.

Children, then, are also constructed as objects of desire in this film. In a sense, the innocence of babies, of children and of sexually uninitiated young women are here virtually equated. But while manifest in certain objects of desire, innocence is at the same time declared unattainable or foredoomed to being lost. Here, perhaps, in the very elusiveness of desire, expressed in a tale of lost innocence, lies the poignancy of *Where Are My Children*. Walton, a morally upstanding man, and his wife, a repentant woman, are nevertheless – because the moral/sexual purity of the world about them has become irretrievably corrupted – visited by the wrath of the gods and condemned together to a lonely and bitter old age. Alone with his wife after discovering what she has done, Walton cries: 'Where are my children?' While her husband continues to grieve 'for his lost children and his lost faith in the woman who should have been their mother', Mrs Walton tries to conceive. But it is too late:

> having perverted Nature so often, she found herself physically unable to wear the diadem of motherhood.

Such a dreadful perversion calls forth retribution so terrible that even the upright and the repentant must be destroyed by it: the punishment accorded Malfit for his assistance in 'race suicide' seems paltry by comparison. The eugenic sermon is swamped by the cinematic melodrama.

As a film 'about' birth control or 'about' eugenics, *Where Are My Children* might well be addressing, as its prologue claims, a serious and intelligent audience. In its construction of the degraded and fecund poor of the first part of the film as unremittingly Other, it also appears to be speaking to a 'respectable', if not a wholly middle-class, audience. It was certainly for these social groups that eugenics as a system of thought had its greatest appeal, and about whom the worst fears about falling birth rates and 'race suicide' were expressed.[20] As a 'quality' film with a moral message, then, *Where Are My Children* undoubtedly aspires to that respectability which the film industry at this period strove ceaselessly to secure for its products. At the same time, though, as a fictional narrative skilfully combining the stylistic conventions of what was soon to become 'classical Hollywood cinema'[21] with the prevailing generic requirements of popular melodrama, *Where Are My Children* was clearly capable of appealing to a much broader audience. In this perhaps lies the secret of the film's success in the US: its status as a 'sermon' assisted in the negotiation of its dangerous passage through the straits of censorship, while its powerful qualities as dramatic cinema pulled in the audiences.

A Hollywood film in Britain: Cinema and social purity

But *Where Are My Children* had an altogether different reception in Britain, where it was exactly its construction as a 'sermon' that prevented the film from reaching large audiences and achieving commercial success. Through the institutional context in which it was introduced, it was constituted as a very particular type of film, in that it was never regarded as

being 'about' anything other than eugenics, or rather – even more specifically – race suicide. Its qualities as a 'good story' – an emotional family
melodrama, a tale of lost innocence, of corruption and retribution – disap-
peared, submerged under a moral message harnessed to a set of anxieties,
prevalent in Britain in the years before and during World War I, about
the decline of the nation.

These concerns expressed themselves in a variety of ways, among them
the fear – with the flower of the nation's youth being destroyed in the
trenches and some of the best of its future mothers apparently more interested in feminist politics than in childbearing – [22] that the population was
deteriorating, both in quality and in quantity. There was a conviction, too,
that the eugenic threat went hand-in-hand with a decline in moral standards, amongst the young especially. Cinema-going, still rather a novelty
and an extremely popular leisure pursuit, was not infrequently held responsible for this state of affairs. Not only were audiences exposed to all the
moral risks associated with darkened, enclosed public places, but many
of the films themselves were thought to be sexually suggestive, or even
incitements to criminal behaviour.

Anxieties such as these are what lie behind the enormous – and sometimes even obsessive – public interest taken at this period in a whole array
of issues relating to sexuality, eugenics included. They also fuelled the
activities of various organisations devoted to the promotion of 'social
purity'. It was under the aegis of one such body, the National Council of
Public Morals, that an influential investigation of the social and moral
influence of cinema – the first of its kind in Britain – was undertaken. This
inquiry was launched soon after the British debut of *Where Are My Children*, also sponsored by the NCPM, which took place on 8 November 1916.
The National Council had a relatively longstanding interest in eugenics,
and a rather more recent one in cinema. Formed in 1911 with the objective
of 'the regeneration of the race – spiritual, moral and physical', as a forum
for public figures concerned with various aspects of 'national degeneration',
this body had launched itself by publishing a 'Manifesto on Public Morals',
signed by a long list of prominent public figures and expressing 'alarm at
the low and degrading views of the racial instinct which are becoming
widely circulated at the present time'. Causes for concern included the
declining birth rate, the circulation of pernicious literature, the moral
education of the young, and the prolific breeding of the 'feeble-minded'.[23]

For the following ten years and more, the National Council of Public
Morals was to be an influential voice in campaigns around social purity,
public morals and social reform. As its inaugural manifesto's references to
the birth rate and to the feeble-minded indicate, the Council's activities
were heavily influenced by the eugenic thinking that coloured so many
public debates at the time. Indeed, in 1913 the NCPM mounted its own
inquiry into the declining birth rate by setting up the National Birth-Rate

Commission, whose report was first published in June 1916. This confirmed that the decline in birth rates was greatest in areas with a high standard of living, and that birth rates fell as incomes rose: in short, that there was a class differential in fertility. This, argued the report, was due to the widespread practice of birth control among the middle and upper classes, and the fact that the lower classes were much less liable to control their fertility in this way:

> While there should be censure of the recklessness of the poor who assume parental responsibility without the capacity or the effort to discharge it worthily, there should be no less condemnation of the selfishness, or social ambition, which leads some of the well-to-do to restrict their families, so that they may make more display, and live in a luxury inconsistent with health and happiness.[24]

Published just as *Where Are My Children* was enjoying its successful first run in New York, this statement more or less sums up the moral message of the film, certainly as the NCPM was to see it.

The Council's interest in *Where Are My Children* seems to have been motivated by the fact that the film could be read as reinforcing the findings of its own Birth-Rate Commission. That this is so is certainly suggested by the ways in which the film was promoted and received in Britain. Every British report or review of the film stressed its character as a 'film sermon': *The Bioscope*, for example, announced it as 'The Birth Limitation Picture', while *The Times* headlined its report of the premiere 'The Cinema and the Birth Rate – a Film for Adults'. The NCPM's director described it as 'a distinct departure from the purely recreative aim of most film-plays. . . . It has a serious purpose and should be a potent factor in social enlightenment'.[25] A prologue and epilogue were even added to the film itself, 'explaining eugenic methods, urging the need of keeping up the population, drawing attention to the work of the National Council. . . .'[26] Among the speakers at the November screening, which was attended by an array of prominent social reformers and public morality campaigners, were the Bishop of Birmingham, President of the NCPM, and the popular writer on eugenic topics, C. W. Saleeby. Both spoke not only about the 'problem' of birth limitation, but also of the potential of cinema for the education and enlightenment of the public. The NCPM's sponsorship of *Where Are My Children*, Saleeby hoped, was 'the beginning of a closer association between those who were working for the morale of the race and those who provided amusement for the public'.[27]

This was the Council's first attempt to use cinema as a means of furthering its objectives, and the venture was undertaken with the full cooperation of the film trade. *Where Are My Children* had been taken up by the NCPM on the initiative of Transatlantic Films, the firm which handled British distribution of Universal pictures. At this stage, Transatlantic

"WHERE ARE MY CHILDREN?"
SPECIAL PROPAGANDA FILM.

SOME LEADING OPINIONS.

THE BISHOP OF BIRMINGHAM.

Speaking to the distinguished company who met him after the recent exhibition of the above film at the Philharmonic Hall, London

(which included amongst others the Duchess of Marlborough, the Bishop of Barking, Lady Emily Lutyens, Rev. Dr. and Mrs. Meyer, Muriel Countess de la Warr, Mr. W. Joynson Hicks, M.P., The Lord Bishop of Birmingham, Mr. John E. Tippett, Lady Willoughby de Broke, Dr. A. Newsholme, C.B., The Lady Sydenham, Principal A. E. Garvie, D.D., Lady Aberconway, Mr. Geoffrey Williams, Sir James Crichton-Browne, D.Sc., F.R.S., Sir Hedley Le Bas, Lady Frampton, Sir George Frampton, Mr. Raymond Green, M.P., Dr. and Mrs. T. W. Kelynack, Canon J. W. Horsley, Lady Butlin, Dr. C. W. Saleeby, Mr. Walter Reynolds, L.C.C., Lady Danvers, Rev. F. C. Spurr, Dr. A. T. Schofield, Rev. T. Rhondda Williams, Rev. Prof. and Mrs. H. Bisseker, Sir John Kirk, Prof. Gollancz, M.A., D.Lit., Lady Glenconner, Lady Cohen, Sir J. M. Godlee, Mr. Travers Buxton, Mr. W. L. Courtney, Mr. Murray Davis, L.D.S., R.S.C., Eng., Sir Bryan Leighton, Capt. C. A. Baragar, C.A.M.C., Lieut.-General Sir A. Codrington, and representatives from The Women's Municipal Party, The Children's Aid Committee, The Association for Moral and Social Hygiene, National Health Society, Conservative and Unionist Women's Franchise Association, Tipperary League, Stepney School for Mothers, National Union of Women's Suffrage Societies, etc.)

His Lordship said "the principle upon which the National Council has conducted its wide operations is to encourage the good things to oust the undesirable. In the world of Literature it is recognised that that has been a wise and effective policy, and we ourselves have found it the best in the long run.

"This film marks an epoch. The Council has long recognised the enormous influence of the Cinema, and has applauded all the efforts it has made to arouse the best patriotism and ideals of the nation at this supreme crisis.

"The problem of the film we have witnessed is one which gravely concerns the Empire. Empty cradles need filling, our Colonies need virile men and women. We must appeal to the heart of the nation, for it is our race, which has done many immortal things for humanity, which is in the gravest danger. This great heritage we must hand on, enhanced in quality, in vigour and in numbers sufficient to enable it to keep its place in the world.

"That is the object of our support of this film—it is to be shown under special conditions, to adults only, and one of the conditions laid down by the Council and fully accepted by the producing company is that all further films which deal with social problems must be submitted to the Council for examination and approval before being shown. We believe Churches, Social Workers, Municipal Authorities and others will welcome our effort, and we appeal to them all to encourage its exhibition for the sake of this great Empire which we all love."

W. JOYNSON HICKS, M.P.

I cannot imagine that your film will do otherwise than good. I know there are certain subjects which, owing to a strain of prudery in the English mind, are kept in the background; but I am convinced that it would be much better for our young people if they were decently and honestly discussed as they are in your film.

Fig. 2 NCPM publicity for *Where Are My Children*

NURSING TIMES.

The play is touching and powerful and should exercise a wholesome influence when shown to adult audiences. We learn that other films are in preparation. They should greatly help in combating the declining birth-rate, especially at a time when Britain will need every available citizen for building up its future after the War.

GLASGOW EVENING NEWS, November 7th, 1916.

The experiment is extremely interesting, and the Council has taken fullest care to guarantee attention; They have arranged the music and taken other means of improving the exhibition.

EVENING STANDARD & ST. JAMES' GAZETTE, November 9th, 1916.

The Bishop, in approving the Cinema presentation of moral lessons, is encouraging a rivalry to the pulpit which the latter will find it difficult to withstand. The moving picture is certainly a greater power than the spoken word, unless the speaker be gifted with uncommon powers of eloquence.

KINEMATOGRAPH AND LANTERN WEEKLY.

Admittedly, the subject is one of the most difficult that any producer could have been asked to handle. It is a Trans-Atlantic film, and it comes to us with all that finished excellence, both in acting and photography, for which the great American firm of film producers enjoys so deservedly high a reputation. But " Where are my Children ?" is something much more than a great picture drama. Rarely, if ever, have we seen so singularly difficult a theme so beautifully, so reverently, so delicately, and so perfectly handled. There is not a single incident in the whole five reels to which the most super-sensitive critic could justifiably take exception. The film cannot fail to deeply impress all who see it.

EVENING NEWS, November 1st, 1916.

The exhibition this week to men and women of science of the film "Where are my Children?"—which, later on, is to be shown to the adult public—marks a big step forward in the moulding of national character through the people's amusements.

Telegrams:
EGRAM, WESTCENT, LONDON."

Telephone
5590 MUSEUM.

National Council of Public Morals
For Great and Greater Britain.

Objects: The Regeneration of the Race—Spiritual—Moral—Physical.

President of National Council:
THE LORD BISHOP OF BIRMINGHAM.

President of the Ladies' Council:
MRS. MARY SCHARLIEB, M.D., M.S. ?

Past Presidents:
THE RT. REV. BISHOP BOYD CARPENTER, K.C.V.O., D.D., D.C.L., D.LIT.
THE LORD BISHOP OF DURHAM.

Chairman of Committee: REV. R. F. HORTON, M.A., D.D.
Vice-Chairman: PRINCIPAL A. E. GARVIE, M.A., D.D.
Hon. Treasurers: PROF. H. GOLLANCZ, M.A., D.LIT. ; REV. F. B. MEYER, B.A., D.D.
Director and Secretary: REV. J. MARCHANT, F.R.S.ED., F.R.A.S.
Solicitors: WONTNER & SONS.
Accountants and Auditors: CARTER, CLAY & LINTOTT.
Bankers: BARCLAY & Co., 54, Lombard Street, E.C.

Headquarters: 20, BEDFORD SQUARE, LONDON, W.C.

wanted the film to be shown in commercial cinemas, but the NCPM, backed by certain sections of the trade, apparently had different plans, regarding it as a purely 'propagandist' picture whose exhibition should be restricted to adults-only audiences in premises acquired expressly for the purpose.[28] If cinema was to enter the domain of social purity, it would do so only under the most strictly controlled conditions.

Where Are My Children, then, was sponsored in Britain by a social purity organisation whose efforts in this sphere enjoyed the blessing of the film trade. But, as the hint of disagreement over exhibition circumstances would suggest, this does not mean that the interests of the two parties necessarily coincided. The NCPM might well have regarded cinema as a suitable vehicle to which to harness its own objectives, but it nevertheless had no intention of directing its message to the masses. It was more interested in those groups in society for whom eugenic ideas would already have some meaning: precisely the intelligent and serious-minded audience that the film itself claims to address. The difference between the American and the British situations was that in Britain this audience was closely targeted, institutionally and discursively, by the construction of the film as 'propagandist' and by its non-commercial exhibition.

Commercial cinemas were frequented by the 'masses' – precisely, it was assumed, the sort of audiences that might be attracted by the film's qualities as a 'good story', or even by a prurient interest in its subject matter, rather than by anything serious it might have to say on the question of race suicide. The sponsors of the film were bent, then, on circumscribing the ways in which it could be read – on fixing its meanings, in other words. The project of directing the film's reading is merely an extension of the insistence on a distinction between the 'recreative' function of the general run of films and this film's loftier objective of moral instruction. And so despite the fact that *Where Are My Children* was a Hollywood product, a commercial feature film intended for commercial exhibition, in Britain it was redefined as a vehicle of enlightenment, a purpose held distinct from that of commercialised leisure and entertainment.

The National Council of Public Morals, then, considered that the cinema screen could be used for 'good and high motives'. This was a view which the film trade was quite prepared, for the moment at least, to endorse, being ever eager to persuade the world that its business was reputable. At the time *Where Are My Children* was being launched in Britain, the film trade was even more anxious than usual to assert its respectability, for in the closing months of 1916 it had, as noted in the last chapter, been under threat of state censorship of films. First publicly mooted in May 1916, the Home Office's plans for official censorship were well advanced by October, when the Home Secretary's proposals for 'an official and independent censorship . . . established by the government' were submitted to the Cabinet.[29] But the Home Office had underestimated the influence and persistence of the film trade, which immediately mounted a public campaign of protest against the proposed measures. This campaign was launched only a week or so before the British premiere of *Where Are My Children*.[30] In lending its support to the NCPM, the film trade was evidently intent on silencing its critics by demonstrating that cinema, widely considered to be a corrupting influence, could actually be put to socially worthwhile uses.

That such a highly respectable body as the National Council of Public Morals had decided to sponsor a film was an indication that cinema was at last being taken seriously. And, as some of the speeches at the launch hinted, there was more to come. Indeed, at the end of November, the NCPM announced its intention of setting up, on the model of the Birth-Rate Commission, a Commission of Inquiry on Cinema, whose terms of reference would be:

1 To institute an inquiry into the physical, social, educational and moral influences of the cinema, with special reference to young people; and into
2 The present position and future development of the cinematograph, with special reference to its social and educational value and possibilities.
3 To investigate the nature and extent of the complaints which have been made against cinematograph exhibitions.
4 To report to the [National Council of Public Morals] the evidence taken, together with its findings and recommendations, which the Council will publish.[31]

The Commission started work almost immediately, receiving evidence from interested parties both within and outside the film trade (though the Home Office declined to participate) until the following May. Its full report, published in October 1917, concluded that worries about the content and influence of films were overstated, if not unfounded, but that care should nevertheless be taken to see that 'suitable' films were shown in 'suitable' conditions. On the question of film censorship, the Commission considered that state censorship would enhance public confidence in the cinema.

However, by the time the report was made public, the censorship situation had already altered dramatically. In early December 1916, the film trade had stepped up its campaign against official censorship by securing the appointment of T. P. O'Connor as new head of the BBFC, a move which coincided with a change of government. The new Home Secretary soon decided, in view of the trade's hostility, to scrap the plans for official censorship of films, and he was also urged by O'Connor to reprieve the BBFC and put it on trial for a year under its new and – it was promised – tougher regime.[32] The Home Office response was not at this stage to give overt support to the Board of Censors but rather to try to persuade local authorities to involve themselves more actively in film censorship. To this end a set of model conditions for cinematograph licences was circulated in January 1917 to all these authorities. They included a clause, the legality of whose import had already been tested in the courts, relating to the moral acceptability of films:

> No film shall be shewn which is likely to be injurious to morality or incite to crime, or to lead to disorder or to be offensive to public feeling. . . .[33]

But although plans for official censorship had been shelved, the possibility that the government might at any moment step in, with or without benefit of legislation, remained. This undoubtedly informed the deliberations, and influenced the conclusions, of the Cinema Commission of Inquiry. It was also to have its effects on the practices of the British Board of Film Censors itself, which – sensing it was very much 'on trial' – displayed extreme caution during this and the following few years. As part of its effort to establish credibility for itself, the new regime at the Board adopted the practice of soliciting advice from the Home Office on films considered especially problematic. *Where Are My Children* was among the first of these.

The film was not actually submitted for censorship until several months after its arrival in Britain, during which time it had been exhibited – though quite how widely it is impossible to tell – in circumstances of the sort favoured by the National Council of Public Morals. For such non-commercial screenings a Censor's certificate would be unnecessary, but perhaps the openings for non-theatrical exhibition had proven limited. For whatever reason, in March 1917 Transatlantic, with the NCPM's support, tried to obtain a Censor's certificate for the film: at some point, therefore, a decision had evidently been made to move it into the commercial sphere. The BBFC's reaction to this request was to ask for Home Office guidance. The Censors felt themselves in difficulty here because although they regarded the film as unacceptable – mainly because of its 'propagandist' purpose, but also because of 'the manner in which the purpose of the film is presented' – they were persuaded that the NCPM's motives in promoting it were above reproach.[34]

It is significant that, in pinpointing the film's purpose – as defined by its sponsors – rather than its content, the Board was in effect colluding with the NCPM's construction of it as 'propagandist'. The BBFC's actions were certainly governed by the view that if the film was censorable, this was not because anything in it was indecent or improper, nor even because it dealt with controversial issues, but simply because it inhabited a problematic category. Faced with a film which aspired to be at once both propagandist and commercial, the Censors were thrown into a quandary. In its resolution of the specific problem posed by *Where Are My Children* the

BBFC, with the support of the Home Office, took the first step towards formulating a policy for resolving future difficulties of the same sort. This policy was to be instrumental in producing and sustaining a discursive separation of the categories 'commercial film' and 'propaganda film'.

In response to the Board's request for advice on *Where Are My Children*, the Home Office took the most unusual step of sending an official to view the film. The Home Office recognised that:

The Censors have hitherto considered films from the point of view of entertainment. If they are to be viewed as a means of inculcating views on morals other considerations would come in and the Board feel that they do not know what they might be led into.[35]

This statement in effect inaugurates a distinction between categories of film contents – entertainment on the one hand, the inculcation of morals ('propaganda', that is) on the other. This distinction was to have significant repercussions for subsequent institutional practices of film censorship, and indeed for the regulation of cinema more generally, and would ultimately underpin a series of discourses on the social function of cinema and its proper place in society.

In the end, the Home Office agreed with the Censors that *Where Are My Children* was not a suitable film to be shown at public performances, even if children were not admitted to it. If, as this and all other available evidence suggests, the Board did in fact refuse to certificate the film, such a decision would mark the birth of a discursive conjunction of entertainment with a public sphere of cinema, one consequence of which was the production of a particular category of films as 'other' – excluded, that is, from the public sphere of cinema. The British Board of Film Censors would eventually, as a matter of policy, decline to certificate all films in the excluded 'propaganda' category, regardless of content (see chapter 4). And the Cinema Commission of Inquiry would – albeit unwittingly – soon be adding its own voice to the Censors' doubts about the advisability of showing in commercial cinemas films dealing with moral and social problems.[36] At any rate, little more was to be heard of the film whose passage through the machinery of censorship had set the whole process in motion.

The birth of the propaganda film

The fate of *Where Are My Children* in Britain is exemplary. The institutional circumscription of its meanings, the insistence on its reading as a film 'about' a particular social problem – race suicide – may be understood on one level in terms of its insertion into pre-existing discourses on eugenics and public morality. At another level, though, the film participates in its own ways in the production of such discourses, engaging narrativity and cinematic modes of address in the process. Thus the film as text does not simply reflect an existing 'social problem', nor even discussions about it in other media: it is itself actively involved in the discursive production and institutionalisation of that problem.[37] When *Where Are My Children* was launched in Britain, moreover, its meanings were harnessed to objectives distinct from any claims on the part of the film text to be a piece of popular fiction cinema: it was in consequence transformed, discursively and institutionally, into a 'propagandist' film, pure and simple.

The discourses and institutions through which this transformation took place were in the first instance those of social purity and public morality. In the shape of *Where Are My Children*, cinema stepped into the domain of public morality at the same moment that public morality, in the shape of the Cinema Commission of Inquiry, entered the domain of cinema. This coincidence of events was not without contradiction, however. On the one hand, cinema was widely regarded as a threat to public morals; on the other, it was seen as a means of spreading moral enlightenment. If the Cinema Commission was a response to the one view, the NCPM's sponsorship of *Where Are My Children* was an expression of the other. But could cinema be at once both a moralising and a demoralising influence?

In terms of a view of cinema as no more than recreation, a popular pastime for the masses, the answer to this question is undoubtedly 'no'. When cinema and public morality entered each other's territory, a struggle ensued over understandings of cinema, its social function and the uses to which it might be put: in short, over what cinema was for. The Cinema Commission's report rehearses exactly these struggles. Was cinema a deleterious moral influence? Did it cause eyestrain and other physical disorders? Were the sorts of films being seen by children of any educational value? As the case of *Where Are My Children* suggests, it was felt in some quarters that cinema might serve useful and worthwhile purposes in ways that might go against the economic and ideological grain of commercialised leisure. That in this one instance at least the entrepreneurs of this leisure pursuit were on the whole in accord with the guardians of public morality only adds further complexity to an already contradictory situation. It was in these circumstances that a film with a certain moral purpose became a film of a particular type, and the propaganda film was born. The union of cinema and public morality, then, produced a new cinematic genre.

But this presented yet more problems. What was the propaganda film's proper place? What – or more crucially, who – was it for? If, in its efforts to gain respectability, the film trade welcomed, for the moment at least, the attentions of the moral reformers, the position of the reformers themselves seems rather less straightforward. On the one hand cinema appeared capable of delivering a large audience for their ideas, on the other, cinema's public image was on the whole somewhat disreputable. If the promotion of *Where Are My Children* is any guide, the moral reformers tried to surmount this problem by addressing themselves, cinematically speaking, to an audience which was much more socially restricted than the usual patrons of commercial cinema – namely, those already in possession of knowledge about the moral and social questions which it was claimed the film was 'about'. If, then, the commercial cinema audience could not constitute the 'ideal readers' of propaganda films, such consumers had to be sought elsewhere. But at this period there was no elsewhere, no institutional space outside commercial cinemas for the public consumption of films. It is this, perhaps, which lies behind the manifest uncertainty of the sponsors of *Where Are My Children* about the 'proper' conditions for the film's exhibition. There was simply no existing institutional structure into which the newly-born genre could slot itself.[38]

If the strategy of mounting private screenings in church halls and similar venues solved the immediate problem of getting the films on the screen, it also kept propaganda films outside cinema's public sphere. The 1909 Cinematograph Act, in subjecting cinema buildings to regulation as places of public resort, already proposed a particular kind of public sphere for cinema. But it is clear from the case of *Where Are My Children* that cinema's public sphere was soon to be defined in terms of particular kinds of films (see chapter 7).

At this point a further contradiction comes into play. In the discourses and practices of film censorship – themselves in a state of flux – in operation at this moment, definitions as to what, in terms of film content, was and was not acceptable were in process of production. These emergent definitions drew upon certain presuppositions about the nature and purpose of cinema: basically, cinema – held to be coterminous with that public domain of cinema which it was the task of censorship to regulate – was already regarded in certain quarters as exclusively 'for' entertainment. The emergence of the propaganda film and its bid to enter the public sphere of cinema constituted a challenge to such a definition, signalling a contradiction – and a rather unlikely one, perhaps, on the face of it – between discourses of public morality and discourses of censorship.

The events surrounding the censorship of *Where Are My Children* highlight the power relations in play at this moment of contradiction. A film with a 'propagandist purpose' could obviously not be assimilated into cinema as it was being constituted in discourses and practices of film censorship. The response of the Censors in the first instance was to suppress this particular film, precisely on grounds of its non-assimilability. In the process, a category called 'propaganda film' was produced in distinction from 'entertainment film'. In the very moment of its production, this new category was – given the equation of the public sphere of cinema with cinema *tout court* – in effect outlawed. The story of *Where Are My Children* in Britain is also the story of how cinema entered the domain of public morality, and vice versa, and of how this resulted in the creation of a film genre which was for some years to inhabit the margins of cinema's public sphere.

4   A Moral Subject

The commonsense of the matter is that a public danger needs a public
warning; and the more public the place, the more effective the
warning.

George Bernard Shaw, 1917

VD propaganda and narrative cinema

If propaganda films came into being as a consequence of a particular
conjunction of cinema and social purity, they survived that union as a
genre, taking up, on their own account, a wide range of social and moral
preoccupations of the day. The propaganda film, which acquired its generic
name at some point between 1917 and 1919, had its heyday towards the
end of, and in the year or two after, World War I. In this brief period, there
appeared in Britain a number of fiction feature films dealing with 'social
problems' of one sort or another, all of them adopting a somewhat similar
approach to a broadly similar set of subject matters. In these films, questions of morality – specifically of sexual morality – are typically dealt with
via an attention to the body, its fitness, and its integrity. They were in fact
sometimes called 'health propaganda' films: in this context the term 'health'
may be understood as a veiled reference to sex.

The body in question in propaganda films is primarily sexual, therefore,
and is constructed as peculiarly vulnerable, especially to such perils as
sexual exploitation and disease. Topics of propaganda films might include
eugenics, birth control, illegitimacy, prostitution or white slavery, but
foremost among the themes of the genre was undoubtedly venereal disease.
During the late 1910s, a number of feature films about VD appeared on
both sides of the Atlantic. These included titles such as *Damaged Goods*
(US, American Film Mfg Co., 1915), *Damaged Goods* (GB, Samuelson
Productions, 1919), *The End of the Road* (US, Public Health Films, 1918),
Fit to Fight (US, Public Health Films, 1919), *Open Your Eyes* (US, Warner
Brothers, 1919), *The Scarlet Trail* (US, John S. Lawrence, 1918), *The
Spreading Evil* (US, James Keane, 1918), *Whatsoever A Man Soweth* (GB,
Beaverbrook, c.1919).

While films of this sort were intended for public exhibition in commercial cinemas, they also claimed to be educational: they were made, said their producers, in order to inform the public about the nature, incidence and consequences of venereal disease. Proponents of such 'propaganda' argued that knowledge about these matters was a good thing in itself, and that disseminating it would help in solving what was regarded as a grave problem for the nation: it was estimated that in Britain as many as one in seven of the population was affected by a sexually transmitted disease. Given the informative function claimed for VD propaganda feature films, it is worthy of note that they are fictional narratives: for in cinema, fiction and information have come to be regarded as mutually exclusive. Although the term 'documentary' was not applied to cinema before the late 1920s, films which would now be called by that name had certainly existed since the very earliest years of the medium. Indeed, during the period under consideration here, documentaries about VD ('lecture films', as they were called) were being made, but these were for use in highly circumscribed non-public contexts – in army training, for instance. The films which attracted attention under the generic label of 'propaganda' were for the most part fictional narratives aimed at broad sections of the cinema-going public.

The medium of fictional narrative and the objective of public availability are united in specific ways in the VD propaganda film. In this instance, cinema as a body of film texts intersects, with certain consequences, cinema as a set of institutions for the production, distribution and exhibition of films. By the late 1910s, the programme of the average commercial cinema consisted typically of at least one fiction feature film with a running time of an hour or more, together with a selection of shorter films – 'topicals', newsreels, travelogues, and the like. The major attraction, though, was already the feature. The twin cornerstones of a rapidly developing new leisure industry were a specific product and a specific mode of consumption: fiction feature films exhibited in purpose-built public cinemas.

During this same period, the fiction film and a particular set of conventions for cinematic narration became hegemonic within the institution of cinema. If fictional narrative was the preferred medium for propaganda films, the choice was in these circumstances strategic – if not necessarily consciously so, and not always with the results presumably intended. Within cinema, a space already existed – together with an audience and an apparatus of reception – for narrative films. Cinematic narrativity organised the reception of films in specific ways, cinema audiences being addressed through their relationship, as spectators, with the ways in which stories were told in films. The physical circumstances of film reception are crucial in this process: by this time, cinema buildings already existed in most localities and were still rapidly growing in number. The pleasure of looking at films could be enjoyed at minimal cost by large sectors of the population. Children and the working classes, it was generally believed, were particularly attracted by this new form of entertainment.

Although the project was not without its contradictions, the VD propaganda film attempted to capitalise on certain aspects of this situation. The objective was to produce films of a sort that could be shown in ordinary commercial cinemas, and so be accessible (in all senses of the word) to a mass audience. In the end, though, VD propaganda films seem to have taken up a marginal position in relation to the mainstream of cinema. This has to do partly with the character of the films themselves, partly with certain institutional constraints upon their accessibility, and partly with the broader social and historical conditions of their production and promotion.

In this chapter, I shall discuss these three sets of factors in turn: taken together, they produce a specific mode of address for the films, an address through which spectators are constructed in a particular way as 'moral subjects'. Such an address, first of all, marks the VD propaganda film, unlike other sorts of propaganda film (*Where Are My Children* being a case in point), as organised according to a textual logic in some respects tangential to that of the mainstream fiction cinema into which it attempted to insert itself. VD propaganda features typically deploy certain of the formal characteristics of 'classical' film narrative: notably an enigma-resolution structure in which conflicts are worked out through the actions of fictional characters and in these characters' relations with one another.[1] Where these films may be said to depart from the classical model is in their tendency to construct characters not as psychologically-rounded individuals, but as representatives, if not of social types, then certainly of moral positions. Moral position is set up here in terms of characters' sexual practices and their placement in relation to a series of discourses centred on the body and its health. Within the fiction, certain of these practices and discourses become privileged over others.

So, for example, the film *Open Your Eyes* (1919) traces the fates of three young men who decide to sow their wild oats, and who all contract syphilis as a result. One goes to an unqualified practitioner for a cure, marries, and has a child born blind. The second also goes to a quack, and passes on the disease to a woman friend. The third goes to a properly qualified doctor and is cured. The second man intends marrying another girl, but the wedding is stopped (for altruistic reasons) by his syphilitic woman friend, who herself undertakes a cure at the hands of the qualified doctor and then marries someone else.[2] In stories of this sort, characters are defined almost completely in terms of their actions: they are what they do. In this particular narrative, characters' actions have straightforward social consequences. Sex of certain kinds leads – inexorably, it seems – to venereal disease. Consulting an unqualified practitioner leads equally inexorably to the spread of infection. Consulting a properly qualified doctor is the only sure way of re-establishing the integrity of the diseased body, and consequently of restoring equilibrium to the world of the fiction, so permitting a resolution of the narrative.

Fit to Fight (1919) has a similar story, this time involving five young men: 'Billy, a college football man; Chick, another [*sic*] rich and rather dissipated college boy; Kid, a pugilist who has lost his title by weakness due to too much drinking, promiscuous association with women, and late hours; Hank, an ignorant country boy who is leaving his country home and rustic parents to seek his fortune in the city; and Jack, a sporting cigar salesman'.[3] When America enters the world war, this cross-section of class types and moral positions finds itself drafted into the Army. All the men receive instruction on venereal disease from their company commander, and each responds to the message according to type.

On leave in town, four of the young men are picked up by prostitutes, Billy being the only one to resist temptation. 'After this evening, Kid, impressed by the Army regulations, takes prophylaxis'. So does Jack, who nevertheless still contracts syphilis, as also does Hank. Billy and Kid alone escape infection. 'The picture ends with Billy and Kid happily leaving for the war front. Back in the hospital are the "useless slackers" who through weakness and disobedience of orders have made themselves a burden upon the government by contracting a venereal disease'. The message is clear: clean living is the only sure way to guarantee the physical integrity necessary to fight for one's country. Contracting VD saps the fibre of the fighting forces, and is profoundly unpatriotic. Again, the points are made by contrasting the actions and fates of characters who occupy different moral positions.

The equation of bodily health, moral purity and fighting fitness applies exclusively to male characters, however. Unlike *Open Your Eyes* and *Fit to Fight*, *The End of the Road* (1919) is aimed at female audiences, though once again the actions and the fates of various characters are counterposed. This story is about two young women who have grown up together in a small town. 'One girl has the right kind of mother who has met her child's inquiries as to the beginning of life with truth. . . . The other girl's mother . . . has ambitions she has never been able to gratify, and whose one idea for her daughter is that she shall make a rich match. . . .' Both young women move to New York, one taking up nursing, the other obtaining employment in a department store. The nurse, 'strengthened by principle and high ideals', refuses a man's advances. The shop assistant, however, accepts the sexual attentions of a man who has no intention of marrying her, thus taking the first step on 'the road that leads in the end to disease, desertion and disgrace'. She contracts syphilis. Meanwhile, the 'good girl' becomes an army nurse, and in the course of her work comes into contact with prostitutes and 'amateurs' in the vicinity of an army camp.

The contrast in moral positions posed between the two female characters in *The End of the Road* motivates documentary or semi-documentary sequences ostensibly conveying information about VD. By way of a lesson, the 'bad girl' is shown exhibits of advanced cases of syphilis by the nurse,[4] who describes preventive measures, and explains how police and social workers may 'save boys and girls from unwise conduct, dangerous to health and morals'. In this film, the disparity in moral position between the two main characters is attributed to aspects of their personal and familial histories, their relationships with their mothers especially. As far as women are concerned, the emphasis is on education, knowledge and prevention – prevention not so much of infection as of sexual activity itself. In a film aimed at female audiences, it is chastity which is presented as the one sure way of avoiding diseases – and disgrace: for active sexuality, disease and disgrace lie in wait together on the only other road open to women.

A limited set of narrative trajectories and resolutions is set up in VD propaganda films, each one representing a particular position on venereal disease, its prevention and its containment. For women, all forms of active sexuality are dangerous; for men, only promiscuous sexual activity is dangerous. Abstaining from sex out of its 'proper' context of marriage and the family is the only certain way, for both men and women, of avoiding infection; though once the damage is done, cure is possible (but for women, 'disgrace' is nevertheless unavoidable). However, cure is by no means an easy route: it can be guaranteed only if sufferers are willing to place themselves in the hands of the right kind of professional person, submitting themselves to an authoritative medical and/or moral discourse. Characters in these stories trace their progress along a circumscribed set of routes through the limited moral positions available to them, at once embodying and reconstructing those positions. What all these fictional VD sufferers have in common, though, is that whatever position they occupy, they suffer a specific – and narratively crucial – lack: that of knowledge. VD propaganda films narrativise the processes through which characters' (and thus spectators') eyes are opened to knowledge, and so to the 'truth'.

To this extent, the various different stories in VD propaganda films express a common theme. The initial problem in the fictional world – the rupture that sets the story in motion – is an absence, in this instance of knowledge. Had the protagonists been aware of the salient facts about venereal disease and its prevention, and had they taken this knowledge to heart before embarking on their sexual adventures, there would have been no stories to tell. This narrativised ignorance, wilful or otherwise, is productive in the sense that it justifies the avowed project of VD propaganda in general and of VD propaganda films in particular: namely, to inform and educate the cinema audience, the public, who are addressed as occupying a precisely identical position of ignorance and moral corruptibility as the characters of the fictions. At the same time, such an address also promises

The End of the Road

*The Story of a Motion
Picture Drama
Prepared for
Women and . Girls
▣▣▣ by the ▣▣▣
War Department*
*Commission on Training Camp Activities
Washington*

Fig. 3 Pressbook publicity for
The End of the Road

that the lack will be filled, that the missing knowledge will be delivered before the story comes to an end.

The 1919 version of *Damaged Goods* is a case in point. This British film was based upon the play of the same name by Eugène Brieux, which had enjoyed considerable success in the West End during the early years of the war. George Dupont, soon to be married to Henriette Louches, discovers that he has contracted syphilis in a casual sexual encounter. He consults a professional practitioner who tells him that a cure will take three or four years and that he must not marry during that time. But his wedding is imminent, and because he can find no plausible excuse for such a long delay, George takes the advice of a quack who promises a cure within six months. The couple marry, and Henriette has a baby which is soon found to be suffering from syphilis. The family consequently discovers George's secret, and Henriette leaves him. At this point, George undertakes a proper cure, and three years later is reunited with wife and child. The story of Edith, the woman who infected George, is also told in some detail: as an employee in a couture house, she had been raped by her boss and sacked when found to be pregnant. By the time George meets her, she has embarked on a career of prostitution in order to pay for her baby's upkeep in an orphanage. Later in the film she turns up again as one of the doctor's 'cases', telling her story to George's father-in-law.

Like the other VD propaganda films, *Damaged Goods* is constructed around a lack of knowledge, notably on the part of George, his mother and his father-in-law. Indeed, all of the characters, with the exception of the doctor, are represented as in some significant respect ignorant or misinformed about VD. The doctor, whose role it is to put the situation to rights, is in consequence crucial – as regards not only the film's characters but also its audience – in the provision of the absent knowledge. If *Damaged Goods* promises to remedy a lack of knowledge, then, it is through the doctor that such a remedy is to be secured. This character is constituted as enunciator: provider of knowledge and speaker of truth.

The 'educational' project of the VD propaganda feature is, then, to narrativise the acquisition of information and knowledge. The fiction film solicits a particular kind of involvement in this process on the spectator's part. Whereas, say, a documentary film of a certain type might implicate the spectator in a didactic rhetoric – the 'facts' would be presented in voice-over, the image would illustrate and thus verify the content of the voice-over[5] – the fiction film embodies a rather less direct mode of address. In the classical narrative, the spectator is typically asked to identify with certain characters and their fates. However, the narratives of VD propaganda films conform only partially to the classical model, in that where identification is solicited, fictional characters occupy a rather different place in the identification process. At this point, the moral positioning proposed by VD propaganda films intercepts the operations of cinematic narrativity.

At the time these films were produced, a particular set of conventions for telling stories by means of the moving photographic image had already become more or less established as the 'right' way to make films. In particular, certain constructions of narrative space and time began to dominate the cinematic image, largely as a consequence of the application of a series of rules governing what would soon be called 'continuity editing'. Continuity editing is a set of techniques for, among other things, matching shots on action, matching the direction of characters' eyelines, punctuating temporal ellipses in stories, and constructing a dissected fictional space intelligible to the spectator. By about 1917, these techniques were widely accepted as constituting the only proper and competent method of putting together fiction films.[6] Many films made during the late 1910s, however, are marked by an unevenness in the application of the continuity system to their construction; or to put it less teleologically, not all films of this period are organised strictly according to the principles of the continuity system. It may also be noted that since the model for classical cinema is generally taken to be the American film, other national cinemas did not necessarily, certainly in this relatively early period, conform in all respects to that model.

In this context, it is of relevance to note that in 1919 the British film *Damaged Goods* was regarded as rather 'old-fashioned' in its style.[7] Many of its sequences, for example, are organised as frontal 'tableau' shots of the sort which characterise earlier forms of cinema,[8] though a tableau-like framing and composition of shots does occasionally persist in films into the 1920s. By about the mid-1910s, however, the tableau was usually functioning simply to establish the space of a particular scene. Such a scene would also contain cut-ins to narratively significant detail and closer framings of characters (at this point, close shots rarely involved much alteration in the camera's angle of view). Silent cinema in general, without the resource of synchronous sound (though, given the regular performance of live musical accompaniment to films in picture palaces, rarely in its time really 'silent'), dealt with speech and dialogue by a mix of expressive acting and written intertitles.

This combination of non-dissected narrative space with extradiegetic sound, a minimum of dialogue, and a maximum expressivity of emotion through gesture and facial expression on the part of a player, is associated with stories and modes of narration prevalent in silent cinema of a certain period: notably with simple, almost folktale-like, melodramas involving 'good' and 'bad' characters constructed as such through iconographies of costume, *mise-en-scène* and gesture. In these films, the camera tends to keep its distance from the action, sustaining a single angle and point-of-view even where a close-up or cut-in signals significant detail or emotion.

A close-up of an actor's face, on which emotions are writ large, marks a particularly dramatic moment. Intertitles function to explain action, to quote dialogue, occasionally even to comment on action or characters.

VD propaganda features occupy a rather uneasy relationship with these conventions of cinematic narration, however. On the one hand, their construction of characters as moral positions – specifically their counterposing, as moral types, of sexually active women and promiscuous men against the chaste and pure of both sexes – may be regarded as quite characteristic of the fiction cinema of the time. In this sense, the VD films' stories are indeed simple enough moral tales. At the same time, though, their simplicity *vis-à-vis* the moral positions they produce is overdetermined by the narrative imperative of rectifying a lack of knowledge. For instance, while iconographic codes might construct a character as morally deficient, the narrative's drive towards knowledge might position that character not as 'bad' so much as merely ignorant or misinformed. Thus in the 1919 version of *Damaged Goods*, George – despite his moment of 'dangerous sexuality' – is presented not as depraved, but rather as a confused young man who has come up against a moral and familial impasse because of his (admittedly rather wilful) ignorance of the true horror of venereal disease. His stricken conscience and moral vacillation are underscored in many an anguished close-up.

In narrative and cinematic terms, the moral positions set against one another in a film like *Damaged Goods* are in effect subsumed to the narrative's logic of rectifying a lack of knowledge. In this film, the doctor, as representative and enunciator of the desired knowledge, assumes a peculiarly privileged position. In the scenes in which he appears, his discourse motivates both image and intertitles. When not shown as part of a setting (surgery, laboratory) connoting professional status and specialised knowledge, this character is typically presented in individual close-up, or in medium two-shot alongside whichever character is at the moment receiving the benefit of his wisdom. Everything about this man's appearance and expression conveys rectitude, sternness, strictness and rigorously unbending correctness. From this elevated position, his enunciation of information – the 'facts' about VD – acquires a peculiarly authoritative quality, as do his instructions and injunctions to other characters (urging George to break off his engagement, for instance) and his sweepingly universalistic statements ('It is the future of the race I am defending').

To the extent that knowledge is not spoken, as it were, directly by the film itself but is mediated instead through a fictional character, the rhetoric of the VD propaganda feature does eschew the didacticism of a direct address to the spectator. At the same time, though, the specifically cinematic aspects of characterisation may operate to some extent to subvert the narrational rhetoric. So, for example, the doctor in *Damaged Goods* functions simply and solely as repository of a knowledgeability and moral

Fig. 4 *Damaged Goods*: the doctor – source of 'proper knowledge' – in his consulting room

rectitude which are first of all reduced to one another, and then expressed in a degree of verbosity which stretches to the limit the capacity of silent cinema to deal with words as opposed to actions and emotions.

In line with their avowed project of disseminating information about sexually transmitted diseases, VD propaganda films at once propose a want of knowledge and offer themselves as a means of filling the gap by providing not merely knowledge, but knowledge of exactly the right sort. The 'correct' knowledge, moreover, is proposed as coming from – spoken from – a particular source. In the case of VD propaganda, knowledge is guaranteed mainly by science, specifically by science harnessed to discourses of medicine and social purity. In this space, the 'correct' knowledge about VD is produced and delivered through the authoritative agency, usually, of properly qualified medical practitioners, though sometimes also by professionals whose brief is public morality – namely, social workers.

So, for example, films like *Open Your Eyes* and *Damaged Goods* (1919) are at pains to distinguish between 'proper' and 'non-proper' knowledge about venereal disease, and to establish a source for the former: the qualified doctor as against the quack. But at the same time, these films also operate within, appeal to, a particular moral universe: the benefits of proper medical and scientific knowledge are represented as by no means easy to come by for the VD sufferer. If George Dupont in *Damaged Goods* has to wait three or four years to be fully cured, this may be regarded as both adequate punishment and sufficient retribution for his sexual transgression. Nor is it by chance that, in the medico-moral discourse of VD

Fig. 5 *Damaged Goods*: 'non-proper' knowledge – George consults a quack

propaganda, cure and salvation are repeatedly conflated. In one especially illuminating exchange, George pleads with the doctor: 'No, no, for pity's sake! You can cure me before that. Science can do everything!' To which the doctor sternly replies: 'Science is not God Almighty (except by prayer). The age of miracles is past.' Despite a refusal to equate science with God or with miraculous cures, the reference to prayer still appeals – if only parenthetically – to a concept of salvation: salvation brought about by one's own efforts as much as by the munificence of the Almighty or even by the blessings of scientific knowledge. More secular metaphors of salvation are invoked, too, in some VD propaganda films: in *The End of the Road*, for example, social workers and police are constructed as possessors of the knowledge and authority that will enable them to '*save* girls and boys from unwise conduct, dangerous to health and morals' (emphasis mine).

The narratives of VD propaganda films produce and circulate discourses centred on knowledges of specific kinds, with particular institutional locations. For instance, they participate in the discursive and institutional construction of public health by authorising – literally by giving authority to – science as a means of securing the health of the public (of the social, as much as of the sexual) body. At the same time, though, the power of science and the rewards of moral virtue are constituted as interdependent. The health of the sexual body serves in some respects as a metaphor for the fitness and moral soundness of the social body. In VD propaganda

Fig. 6 *Damaged Goods*: 'No, no, for pity's sake! You can cure me before that. Science can do everything!'

Fig. 7 *Damaged Goods*: 'Science is not God Almighty. . . . The age of miracles is past.'

features this is commonly expressed in a preoccupation with the integrity of the family in society.

Thus in *Damaged Goods*, and to a certain extent also in *Open Your Eyes*, the virulent contagiousness of VD is set up as a direct and ever-present threat – not only within the area of illicit and 'dangerous' sexual practices, but also to that sphere *par excellence* of clean and socially acceptable sex, marriage and the family. In *Open Your Eyes*, the man who goes to a quack to be cured of syphilis and then marries has a child born blind. This affliction of the family, it may be inferred, is a direct result of – if not a punishment for – his failure to seek knowledge in the right quarter and so obtain a proper cure for his disease. A similar fate befalls the Dupont family in *Damaged Goods*: not only are George's innocent wife and child infected with syphilis, but the baby's wetnurse is in danger of contracting the disease as well. The 'sins of the fathers' referred to in one of the film's intertitles have clearly returned to roost within this particular family. Again, moral and medical discourses are elided. In a cut-in close-up of a biblical extract, reference is made once again to sin:

Against thee, thee only have I sinned . . . be clear when thou judgest.

If the integrity of the family is to be restored, both disease and sin must be purged.

The final scene of *Damaged Goods* marks the end of George's three-year cure and expiation. In an emblematic moment of closure for popular fiction cinema, George, Henriette and the child are reunited, while the doctor proclaims: 'Whom God hath joined, let no man put asunder.' In the film's closing moment, George holds the child in one arm, puts the other around his wife, and kisses both of them. If George's disease and failure to have it cured are brought about by a lack of knowledge which results in the break-up of his family, a full restoration of the situation and a resolution of the film's narrative must entail a cure of the disease and a reconstitution of the family. Both of these are brought about by the agency of the doctor as repository of proper knowledge, and sealed by his positively priestly blessing.

If the 'family romance' has been a staple of narrative cinema from its earliest years,[9] VD propaganda films – where they construct stories around heterosexual courtship, sex, marriage and family life – take up this preoccupation. The specificity of these films, however, lies in their proposal of 'improper' sexual conduct and the ensuing physical disorder as a particular kind of threat to the integrity of the family. In this respect they depart somewhat from the characteristic 'family romance' of mainstream silent cinema. Some VD propaganda films, however, forgo the 'family romance' altogether, thus placing themselves at yet greater distance from the preoccupations of contemporary fiction cinema.

The theme of *Fit to Fight*, for example, is not so much the integrity of

Fig. 8 *Damaged Goods*: 'The End' – disease cured and family reunited

the family as that of the nation, as represented by its fighting forces, in time of war. To this extent, the film is caught up in a particular set of discourses circulating outside cinema itself, discourses which are produced also through other representations and institutions, and which produce notions of 'patriotism'. Such a passage across discursive practices is by no means unproblematic, however. In this film, moral positions are constructed around the contrast between men who are fighting fit because they do not have VD, and 'useless slackers' infected by disease and in consequence unable to go to the front. However, it might be that neither syphilis nor possible death in the trenches would present itself as a particularly attractive alternative to the audiences at which the film was directed: this might introduce an element of instability into the reception of this fiction film as a piece of instruction. One thing which *is* abundantly clear in *Fit to Fight*, though, is that it is women, or women of a certain kind, who are at the root of the trouble: the soldiers are urged by their officer to 'keep away from prostitutes as the only sure way of avoiding a venereal disease'.

Such a preoccupation with the troublesome consequences of certain manifestations of female sexuality is entirely characteristic of the VD propaganda genre. In *The End of the Road*, a film aimed at a female audience, the moral lesson is intended to appeal to a 'woman's point of view'. The background of the 'bad girl' and the circumstances of her 'fall' are set out

Fig. 9 The woman's fall from sexual innocence to disgrace: Edith (in *Damaged Goods*) relives her ordeal

before the inexorable consequences of disease, desertion and disgrace ensue. Similarly – and significantly, given the character's marginality in the original play – Edith's story of seduction and desertion is told at some length in the 1919 version of *Damaged Goods*. In all these films, there is a certain fascination with the moment of a woman's fall from sexual innocence to disgrace (there being no intermediate possibilities posed). This preoccupation in fact pervades the fiction cinema of the period: women are typically constructed as essentially pure and innocent, but infinitely morally corruptible; once initiated into extramarital sex, disgrace inevitably follows for them. In the VD propaganda feature, specifically, it seems to be sexual initiation as much as the disease itself that brings about a woman's downfall. In a film like *The End of the Road*, the only effective way proposed for women to avoid such a downfall is foreknowledge: armed with proper sex education and the lofty moral principles learned from her mother, the 'good girl' avoids a terrible fate and is thus able, in her capacity as a nurse, to be of service to society. Later, it is implied, she in her turn will be a good wife and mother.

VD propaganda films, with whatever degree of sympathy, construct sexually active women as the principal cause of venereal infection. This is effected within a set of discursive constructions of female sexuality which operate to distinguish it from male sexuality. Women are fundamentally innocent, but extremely vulnerable to corruption at the hands of men. At the moment of corruption, though, women immediately lose all vestiges of purity and become dangerous – to themselves as well as to men. Men, on the other hand, are not basically pure and innocent, nor are they automatically disgraced by sexual initiation. Sex in an 'improper' – that is, in a non-marital – context may involve risks of other kinds for them, but these can be avoided by chastity ('clean living') or minimised by a healthy respect for medical expertise.

Discourses around female and male sexuality are constructed through VD propaganda films in their deployment of cinematic signifiers and modes of narration which also operate across other types of fiction cinema of the period: these include certain codes of characterisation and a narrativisation of female innocence and its ever-threatened loss. At the same time, though, these representations draw upon and recirculate contemporary social discourses which also operate outside of cinema. A similar argument might also be advanced concerning representations of the family both within and outside the cinema of the period, and also – though perhaps less straightforwardly – about discourses on nationhood, on the health, quality and integrity of 'the race'.[10] This indicates that an attention to film texts, though productive, does not exhaust analysis of the processes by which social discourses around sexuality, morality, health and nationhood are circulated in VD propaganda features, for such discourses do not inhabit films alone.

The VD film, censorship and social purity

When the British version of *Damaged Goods* was previewed to the film trade in London late in 1919, the occasion – which included a luncheon and speeches by various public figures – provided an opportunity to contrast the achievements of the native cinema with those of an American film industry whose products were already dominating British cinema screens, One speaker compared the film favourably with an unnamed recent American offering on the same topic (most probably *The End of the Road*), saying that where 'the American production dealt with the subject in all its ugliness and almost vulgarity', the British film was distinguished by 'its artistic qualities and the display of taste'.[11] Although a distinction between the vulgarity of American cinema and the tastefulness of the home product has repeatedly been appealed to in defence of British cinema, it has a particular resonance in this instance.

The negative criticisms of the American film are undoubtedly an allusion to its explicit representation of the 'horrors' of VD, as, for instance, in the quasi-documentary sequences in which the 'bad girl' is shown exhibits of cases of syphilis. Such a tactic was not confined to this particular film; on the contrary, it seems to have been a distinguishing mark of the VD propaganda genre. It can be traced as far back at least as the (American) 1915 version of *Damaged Goods*, in which George is shown pictures in a medical textbook of the effects of VD on its victims, and witnesses a medical lecture in which syphilis sufferers are put on display. Such graphic illustrations excited a good deal of condemnation in Britain. *The Times* review of *The End of the Road*, for instance, calls one or two incidents in the film 'revolting', while a reviewer of the same film in the Association of Social and Moral Hygiene's journal *The Shield* contends that the horrors of VD had already been pressed too much. Another American film, *Open Your Eyes*, was similarly criticised. Photographs of the effects of diseases, said one reviewer, 'cultivate an unhealthy taste for horrors', and appeal to a 'public taste for dwelling on horrors and disease, a morbid taste fostered by the war'.[12]

By contrast with the alleged sensationalism of the American VD films, the British *Damaged Goods* aspired to sell itself as a piece of 'quality' cinema. Its treatment of sensitive subject matter is ostentatiously 'restrained': information about sexually transmitted diseases which might be conveyed visually in other VD propaganda films is here communicated through the doctor's speeches, in the long intertitles already referred to. However, the film was regarded at the time it was made as lacking in the qualities which would make it good cinema ('from the point of view of screen art', said one commentator, 'it is not good'),[13] precisely because, in its refusal to construct VD as a spectacle, it failed to capitalise on cinema's potential as a visual medium.

The issue of the cinematic qualities of VD propaganda features links with the question of what these films were intended to do, by whom, and for whom. It seems clear that, in Britain at least, efforts were made to promote them on the basis of their educative value. In textual terms, to the extent that their narratives aim to rectify a certain lack of knowledge, they do indeed deliver on such a promise. The educational project is institutionally implicated as well, in that VD propaganda films were sometimes sponsored and/or promoted by social purity and social reform organisations. Particularly active in this sphere was the National Council for Combating Venereal Disease, founded by Lord Sydenham of Combe, Chair of the Royal Commission on Venereal Diseases.[14] *The End of the Road*, for example, was 'approved' by the NCCVD (and by the newly-formed Ministry of Health). The precise nature of the relationship between such organisations as the National Council and producers of VD propaganda features is not so clear, however. For example, although Lord Sydenham, in a private letter written in 1917 to the Home Secretary, expressed the view that a film version of *Damaged Goods* would be a worthwhile project,[15] there is no evidence of NCCVD backing or support for the film either during or after its production. The film was apparently produced as a purely commercial venture.

With their somewhat indeterminate relationship with social purity and social reform, VD propaganda films entered the arena of exhibition in a slightly anomalous manner. They might, as in the case of the launch of *Damaged Goods*, be showcased at special private screenings sponsored by social purity groups, with attendant publicity and announcements to the effect that they were not for exhibition in commercial cinemas.[16] At the same time, some at least were screened in public cinemas as well: this is certainly true, for example, of *Damaged Goods* and *The End of the Road*. However, the commercial exhibition of VD propaganda films was mediated by various conditions, foremost among which were undoubtedly institutions and practices of film censorship.

When 'propaganda' features – not only VD films but also films dealing with other social problems – began to make an impact, the BBFC was thrown into a quandary. It eventually resolved its dilemma by deciding, as a matter of policy, to refuse certificates *a priori* to all propaganda films: not – significantly enough – on grounds that such films might be 'indecorous', but because the cinema was, according to the Board, not a suitable place to air matters of potential controversy. The BBFC's treatment of the pro-eugenics feature *Where Are My Children*, discussed in the previous chapter, suggests that in 1917 a distinction between education and entertainment was already emerging in relation to cinema. A film could inhabit one or other, but never simultaneously both, of these categories, and only members of the latter were considered suitable for exhibition in commercial cinemas. Cinemas, in other words, were seen as exclusively for 'entertainment' films, and entertainment films were to be neither educational nor controversial. In 1919, in response to the rash of VD propaganda films, the Board of Censors sent a circular letter to film producers and distributors explaining its policy of withholding certificates from all propaganda features. These films, it was stated, were unsuitable for public commercial exhibition and were better viewed in halls specially taken for the purpose, 'where securities could be taken for choosing the audience which are impossible in the ordinary cinema'.[17]

In authorising a policy of refusing to certificate certain films for public exhibition, this discourse places these films outside the domain of mainstream commercial cinema. At the same time, particular formulae of audience and viewing context for different types of film are effectively sanctioned, even privileged: specifically, commercial cinemas, the mass of the film-going public, and 'entertainment' are seen as going hand-in-hand. The BBFC's practices were geared wholly to this model of the cinema and its audiences – a model endorsed, moreover, by the Home Office. When Lord Sydenham of the NCCVD offered his support for the idea of a film version of *Damaged Goods*, he had contended that 'the film would reach an audience

that the play could not touch and . . . good might result'. But as far as the
Home Office was concerned, the popular appeal of cinema was precisely
the problem. A film outside the entertainment category could never be
regarded as appropriate fare for the regular cinema audience, because

> . . . the Cinema differs greatly from the Theatre: the audience is less
> intelligent and educated and includes far more children and young
> people.[18]

The inappropriateness of propaganda films for commercial exhibition is
explicitly (though not publicly) justified in terms of the class, as well as
the age, composition of the cinema audience.

But a policy of refusing certification to a particular group of films may
have unexpected consequences. In this instance, it is exactly through such a
policy that propaganda films were created as a category apart. A discursive
practice was instrumental, in other words, in the constitution of a film
genre: in this sense, censorship has obviously been productive. At the
same time, within the complex configuration of institutions and practices
surrounding the censorship of films during the 1910s, the policies of the
BBFC – scarcely, as I have indicated, authoritative or determining at this
point – were capable of producing effects contrary to those intended. For
one thing, whatever the Board recommended with regard to particular
films or groups of films, the power to permit or prohibit their exhibition
rested in the final instance with local licensing authorities: and many
authorities were at this period quite prepared to ignore any recommendations the BBFC might choose to make.

This, perhaps, explains how – despite the BBFC's Home Office-backed
threats of refusing certification – a British film version of *Damaged Goods*
came to be made in 1919, evidently for commercial release. With an uncertificated film, a distributor could, depending on the conditions attaching to
local cinema licences, approach individual licensing authorities to seek
permission to exhibit in particular areas. Producers, distributors, exhibitors
or sponsors might nevertheless try to impose conditions on a film's public
exhibition. So, for example, *The End of the Road* was announced on its
release to be available for exhibition in cinemas, but only provided that no
children under 14 were present and the film was not shown in conjunction
with another, 'ordinary', feature. Advertisements for this film, too, were to
be approved by its sponsor, the NCCVD. *The End of the Road* was in fact
never submitted to the Board of Censors.[19]

Since the BBFC's powers to discourage local authorities from allowing
public exhibitions of uncertificated films were limited, VD propaganda
features were shown in commercial cinemas up and down the country
(though quite how widely it is impossible to tell). This continued even after
the distribution and exhibition arms of the cinema industry weighed in
with their own bid to suppress the films: early in 1919, the Cinematograph

Exhibitors' Associaton recommended that propaganda films should not be screened for commercial purposes and later attempted to persuade its members not to book *Damaged Goods*.[20] But less than half of all cinema proprietors in Britain belonged to the CEA, and public screenings of this and other propaganda films continued.

Local responses varied: while some licensing authorities permitted propaganda films to be exhibited in commercial cinemas in the normal way, others banned them outright, while yet others imposed special conditions upon their public exhibition, or restricted screenings to specialised non-public venues such as Mechanics' Institutes.[21] Where VD propaganda features were exhibited, then, they were screened in public cinemas in scattered localities in defiance of the recommendations of the BBFC and of the more 'respectable' elements of the film trade; otherwise they were shown in special halls of the sort favoured by the Board, often under the aegis of a social purity or social reform organisation.

The attraction of reaching large numbers of people notwithstanding, the commercial exhibition of VD propaganda features remained something of a problem for their supporters within the social purity movement. In these circumstances, reception became rather a haphazard business: since outside sponsors were rarely in a position to control either publicity or audience composition in the commercial sector, 'intended' readings could by no means be ensured. Cinema proprietors with an eye to profit, for instance, were not above exploiting the sensation value of VD films to attract audiences.

Lurid publicity, restricting admission to persons above a certain age (at a time when in most places there were no age restrictions on admission to films), alternating women-only and men-only screenings – all these tactics for dealing with exhibitions of propaganda films must undoubtedly have suggested an element of the forbidden to the film-going public. As one (anti-censorship) commentator was later to remark on observing the behaviour of cinema-goers queuing to see propaganda films: 'one has only to listen to the conversations of many of these people who believe they are going to see something frankly pornographic.'[22]

The problem about exhibiting propaganda films in commercial cinemas, though, really had less to do with their content than with their audience. In certain crucial respects, discourses of the BBFC, of the Home Office, even of the film trade itself, constructed cinema and its social function basically in class terms. Once a distinction between entertainment and non-entertainment cinema along implicitly class lines – in terms of the class composition of cinema audiences, that is – had been produced and put into circulation, it was recognised that 'intended' readings of films could not be guaranteed, most especially in circumstances where the entertainment/non-entertainment distinction threatened to break down. Since exhibitions of propaganda films in commercial cinemas might constitute a confusion of these carefully distinguished categories, they were evidently to be deplored. Although the Board of Censors was not alone in condemning this practice, the position of propaganda features in relation to discourses surrounding film censorship is an important condition of their marginality with regard to mainstream cinema.

But the situation, certainly in 1919, was perhaps more contradictory than this analysis might suggest. For despite the effectivity of what might be called discourses of categorisation, there was nevertheless a movement towards, a space opened up for, resistance to such discourses. On a very general level, precisely those relations of power which marginalised propaganda films *vis-à-vis* mainstream cinema also constituted an incitement to discourse around their subject matter, namely – broadly speaking – the body and its sexuality. That is to say, there is an incitement if not to the actual production of films on 'propaganda' topics, certainly to modes of reception of such films which would go against the grain of their purportedly 'educational' objectives.

More specifically, space for such 'resistant' readings is opened up within the film texts themselves, through the deployment of strategies of cinematic narration already established in the mainstream popular fiction film. In terms of theme and style, propaganda features did not on the whole differ enormously from the standard fare of commercial cinemas, and in this respect might not have appeared wildly out of place in such a context. Resistance has institutional aspects here as well, though. Indeterminate and at times antagonistic relations between the Home Office, the Board of Censors and local authorities furnished an opportunity which could be grasped on the one hand by elements in the film trade motivated by financial gain – or even social concern – to produce and promote propaganda films, and on the other by social purity organisations aspiring to get their message across to broad sections of the public, even if the interests of these two groups did not necessarily coincide.

Nor indeed was there unanimity within the social purity and social reform movements themselves as to the value of propaganda films. In the National Council for Combating Venereal Disease, widespread dissemination of information on sexual matters appears to have been regarded more or less unquestionably as a good thing. The NCCVD clearly aimed to address itself directly to the public, particularly to the working-class public: its endorsement of cinema as a propaganda vehicle was precisely due to the large, and largely working-class, audience the medium could command.

This, however, was exactly the basis of objections on the part of other social puritans and reformers, many of whom were disdainful of cinema – an attitude, ironically enough, which had a great deal to do with the class composition of the cinema audience. But it was also felt that cinemas were dangerous places, because the conditions (darkness, the proximity of strangers, and so on) in which films were viewed, not to mention the supposedly questionable content of a great many of them, constituted moral risks in themselves. To use commercial cinema for propaganda purposes might, from this point of view, turn out to be a self-defeating manoeuvre.

As noted in the previous chapter, the social purity movement at this period was a site of struggle over understandings of cinema: was cinema to be seen as a threat to public morals, or as a means of spreading moral enlightenment? Such uncertainties might well underlie criticisms of some of the ways in which the moral messages of propaganda films were articulated – notably of the virtually routine inclusion in VD films of visually explicit sequences detailing the horrors of syphilis and other sexually transmitted diseases. 'Constructive moral teaching', argued one feminist moral reformer with reference to this tactic, might in the end prove more effective than scaring people.[23] As time passed, the social purity movement became increasingly cautious about the commercial exhibition of propaganda films. The National Council for Public Morals, for example, after a brief flirtation with cinema in the shape of its sponsorship of *Where Are My Children*, appears to have abandoned its endeavours in this area, whereas the NCCVD (which in 1925 changed its name to the British Social Hygiene Council) held to its pro-propaganda position well into the 1930s.

Nevertheless, even after the mid-1920s, when a degree of national uniformity in censorship practices had been brought about and the BBFC's decisions were much more widely accepted by local authorities, propaganda films continued to be shown in commercial cinemas. Indeed, at a certain point the practice became to some extent institutionalised: while the BBFC continued to refuse certification, many local authorities devised special arrangements for dealing with applications to show propaganda films in their areas.[24] In a 1929 speech, Ivor Montagu, a noted campaigner against the political censorship of films, paints a picture of the propaganda feature as a thriving and profitable sideline for the film trade:

> ... the only films which it is possible to distribute without leave of the
> Board of Censors are lurid and highly-coloured melodramas, which
> by their very flamboyance are capable of earning tens of thousands of
> pounds, such as *The End of the Road* dealing with venereal disease and
> *The White Slave Trade*.[25]

A divergence of interest between the film trade on the one hand and the social purity movement on the other emerges at this juncture. The increasing scepticism of the latter about the value, for its purposes, of commercial exhibition of propaganda films was bolstered by some quite sophisticated audience research. In the early 1930s, for example, one social purity organisation (the National Vigilance Association) was advised by another (the American Social Hygiene Association) that commercial exhibition of propaganda films was not a good idea, 'because in spite of all possible safeguards in advance ... it has been found that sensational publicity for advertising purposes, and the consequent opposition of certain civic and religious groups, have resulted'.

The problem with commercial screenings lay not just with the frequently 'sex-exciting' character of publicity for the films, but also with the difficulty of ensuring that they would be read for their 'social hygiene' content and not be of 'pornographic interest to their audiences'. Limits to the instability of meaning in these texts could, it was felt, be imposed only by tightly controlling the conditions of their reception. Propaganda films, therefore, were best shown non-commercially:

> ... under the auspices of ... organisations interested in social hygiene, or reputable individuals. Audiences are usually selected groups. ...
> [A] speaker explains and supplements the important points made in the picture.[26]

This advice was based on the findings of an American investigation, undertaken in 1922, of the effects on audiences of the VD propaganda film *Fit to Fight*. The researchers expressed doubts about the effectiveness of fictional narrative in this type of film, and stressed the crucial roles of exhibition context and audience composition in their reception.[27]

Although never articulated in these terms, it is clear that, as far as social purity organisations were concerned, the instability of propaganda films as bearers of meaning was a major drawback. In particular the films' position within, or on the margins of, most institutions and some textual operations of mainstream commercial cinema opened them up to unintended and, from the point of view of social purity, 'undesirable' readings. Arguing against propaganda films, one social puritan attributed this undesirability to the fundamentally erotic character of the pleasures of fiction cinema:

> ... instead of affecting the mind, and still less so the heart, [film dramas] affect the nerves, and, above all, the sexual instincts. ... In that lies the mysterious secret of the astonishing success of the cinemas.[28]

Aside from the pleasurable qualities of spectator-text relations in cinema, it can also be argued in the specific case of VD propaganda features that an important condition of unintended readings is precisely those practices of censorship which marginalised the films *vis-à-vis* commercial cinema, and at the same time produced special conditions for their exhibition and reception.

VD propaganda features continued to be made long after the disappearance of the circumstances in which they first emerged. They were certainly being produced and commercially exhibited well into the 1930s: a film called *Damaged Lives* was made in 1933 by Hollywood B-movie director Edgar G. Ulmer, and *Marriage Forbidden*, an American remake of

Damaged Goods, was released in Britain in 1938 under the auspices of the British Social Hygiene Council.[29] Such durability is perhaps to be explained by the peculiar capacity of propaganda films to sustain a range of different readings. By the 1930s, they had acquired their own institutional niche as well as their own 'aberrant' readings. Both of these transcend the social conditions under which the VD propaganda feature made its initial appearance.

A moral panic: The place of cinema

At the moment in the late 1910s when propaganda films acquired their generic title and a number of fiction features dealing with VD appeared, a moral panic about venereal diseases, and syphilis in particular – its high incidence, its enormous contagiousness, its dreadful consequences – was raging, both in Britain and elsewhere. In 1913, a Royal Commission had been set up to look into the question. By 1916, when the Commission's report was published, Britain was two years into war, and the problem seemed even worse than before. It was not simply that venereal disease was much more widespread than had been supposed: according to the Royal Commission, it also had 'grave and far-reaching effects . . . upon the individual and the race'. The findings of the Commission were widely publicised, and the suggestion that, as a preventive measure, 'the young should be taught to lead a chaste life as the only certain way of avoiding infection'[30] was enthusiastically received.

The Report of the Royal Commission on Venereal Diseases produced a discourse on nationhood, sexuality and public morality which was to be a crucial component of the moral panic following on its publication. This discourse – reconstructed, recirculated and modified across a variety of representations over several years – effects a conflation of disease with the state of the British nation, the 'race'. Fears that the race was in decline were prompted in part by the concrete threat to its integrity from without by the enemy. But overdetermining such fears were anxieties about changes in social and sexual mores – the temporary break-up of families, and the equally temporary emancipation of women – in time of war. All these are condensed in a moral panic about diseases, specifically – and not by chance – about sexually-transmitted disorders that were virtually incurable, could spread invisibly and uncontrollably, and have terrible social consequences. At a particular moment, then, a discursive conflation of the moral and spiritual state of the nation with its physical health, with the fitness of the national body, combined itself with fears about uncontained sexuality to produce a moral panic with venereal disease as its focus.[31]

VD propaganda films were not merely an effect of this moral panic, however: they were caught up in it, actively and independently constructing, reconstructing and circulating discourses, as well as drawing upon wider social discourses. The latter is evident especially in the preoccupation of individual films with the threat posed by VD to the family, with the state of 'the race', and with the need for the country's fighting men to keep themselves fit in body and soul by avoiding contagion. To the extent that these films claim to be educative, they participate also in discourses of sex reform, discourses which constituted widespread knowledge about VD as a crucially necessary – if not a sufficient – condition for its control:

Continuous and consistent efforts will be required to keep the complex question of venereal disease before the public mind. . . .[32]

In this particular quest for knowledge, the 'problem' is constantly reinvoked – as if such repetitiveness, instead of fuelling a moral panic, could hope to eradicate its causes.

In contemporary comments on VD propaganda films, as well as in the films themselves, the desirability of 'frankness' in these matters is frequently alluded to. In this respect, VD propaganda films may be seen as participating in an incitement to discourse on sexuality: they certainly recirculate discourses in operation in media – government reports, newspapers, and so on – outside of cinema itself. At the same time, though, as fiction films deploying modes of representation and address peculiar to cinema and drawing upon broader cultural conventions of narrativity, they mediate, modify and reconstruct these discourses in their own ways.

So, for instance, VD propaganda features constitute their spectators as moral subjects by constructing moral positions for their fictional characters, address spectators as lacking in knowledge and promise to rectify that lack, and claim to rectify the lack by constructing the acquisition of knowledge as coterminous with narrative closure. In the course of all this, they draw upon and rework on the one hand discourses of social reform and social purity, and on the other codes of narrative cinema, to position their moral subjects in certain ways: notably as either male or female and as occupying particular positions with regard to sexuality, sexual practices, innocence/corruption, and 'dangerous sexualities'.

The morally-positioned spectators of VD propaganda films were, however, also historical subjects, also a social audience. Since audiences for cinema during this period were widely, and probably accurately, believed to be predominantly working class, it might perhaps be suggested that VD propaganda films participate in that process named by Michel Foucault the 'moralisation of the poorer classes',[33] a specific deployment of sexuality as an instrument of power. Foucault argues that 'bio-power' – the constitution of the body as a site of the expression of power – is manifest in the correlation of a 'racism of expansion' with a concern with the (sexual) body as strong, vigorous and healthy. Not only, in other words, may the health of the nation be seen simultaneously in physical and in sexual terms, but relations of class may also be at stake in these representations.

The foregoing analysis suggests, however, that while VD propaganda feature films might indeed be caught up in these discursive productions, their involvement is not necessarily straightforward. For example, to the extent that they deploy pre-existing conventions of cinematic representation and cinematic narrativity, these films might be seen as more readily constructing the family than the race. While this obviously does not preclude the possibility of the one standing in for the other, it does suggest a certain complexity in relations between discourses and powers in this area. What, moreover, is to be made of the observation that VD propaganda features could be regarded simultaneously as a source of moral enlightenment and as an instrument of moral corruption? This, at the very least, signals a fluidity in meanings and suggests that these films could generate a range of readings – including, perhaps, 'pornographic' ones.

But readings do not emerge from texts alone. As the sponsors of VD films within the social purity movement soon discovered, readings of films are governed by the conditions of their reception. Or to put it another way, readings are generated across, are actively implicated in, an entire apparatus of discourses, practices and powers. Practices of film censorship propose a particular construction of VD propaganda films: namely, that these films are to be regarded not as entertainment for the mass of the cinema-going public, but as education and uplift for the few. Nevertheless, they managed to elude this construction: when exhibited commercially and exploited as in some sense 'other' by virtue of unusual conditions of exhibition and special status as objects of censorship, VD propaganda films provoked different – perhaps even resistant – readings. Thus if film censorship produced the propaganda genre, it also incited the very readings of propaganda films it sought to prohibit. That censorship can be instrumental in the production of certain kinds of readings of films is also demonstrated in the next case history.

5   Pleasure, Prevention and Productivity

If through a mist of awful fears
Your mind in anguish gropes
Dry up your panic-stricken tears
And fly to Dr Stopes.

If you have missed life's shining goal
And mixed with sex perverts and dopes
For normal soap to cleanse your soul
Apply to Marie Stopes.

And if perhaps you fail all round
And lie among your shattered hopes
Just raise your body from the ground
And *crawl* to Marie Stopes.

                              Noel Coward, 1922

From *Married Love* to *Maisie's Marriage*

Maisie Burrows, the eldest of ten children, meets and falls in love with
Dick Reading, a fireman. When Dick proposes marriage, Maisie refuses
him because she cannot face an existence like that of her parents, who
have too many children and not enough money. Turned out of home by
her father after a family row, Maisie wanders the streets in desperation,
eventually attempting suicide by jumping off a bridge. She is rescued, but
immediately arrested and sent to jail for two months. On her release,
Maisie is taken in as a maidservant by her rescuer's wife, Mrs Sterling.
The Sterlings have three children and a blissfully happy marriage, and
from Mrs Sterling Maisie learns that she can enjoy married love without
the consequences she fears. One evening, when Maisie is alone in the house
with the Sterling children, her degenerate brother calls and extorts money.
In the ensuing fracas, the house catches fire and Maisie is rescued by Dick.
The couple, joyously reunited, marry.

This, in brief, is the story of *Maisie's Marriage*, a British film made
and released in 1923. Besides being a love story of a kind undoubtedly
commonplace enough in the popular cinema of the day, *Maisie's Marriage*

also deals – implicitly at least – with birth control and marital happiness, proposing a causal link between the two. Such matters were the subject of extensive debate and much controversy in the early 1920s: the year 1923 in particular was in a number of respects a key moment in the politics of birth control in Britain.

In the early 1920s, the birth control movement had entered a new phase, having begun to secure a broader base of support for its objectives than it had hitherto enjoyed. One of its new goals was to persaude government and local authorities to sponsor clinics dispensing advice and contraceptives: the first birth control clinics in Britain, which were private, had opened in 1921. Arguments in favour of birth control began to emphasise its benefits in terms of the health, welfare and general happiness of mothers and children, a shift away from the earlier, predominantly eugenic, emphasis on the quality of the 'race'. The movement was now ready to make a bid for party political backing, or at least for a voice in Parliament. Although no party ever did actually formulate a policy on birth control, a number of individual MPs were publicly supportive of the cause. Outside Parliament, the movement was also gaining ground within the Labour Party: the idea of birth control as a public health issue was certainly more attractive to the Left than had been the more characteristically middle-class eugenic approach. During this period a number of Labour-controlled local authorities came into conflict with the government over the question of publicly funded birth control clinics.

At the beginning of 1923, public awareness of all these issues was heightened spectacularly by a handful of *causes célèbres*. A health visitor, Nurse E. S. Daniels, was suspended and later dismissed from her job for giving advice on birth control to a number of her clients. The case aroused a great deal of interest and much support for Nurse Daniels herself. At about the same time, two left-wing birth control activists, Rose Witcop and Guy Aldred, were prosecuted for circulating Margaret Sanger's pamphlet, *Family Limitation*, and found guilty of selling an obscene publication. And finally, in February, eugenist, best-selling author and well-known birth control campaigner Marie Stopes went to court with a much-publicised libel suit.[1]

If the appearance of a film like *Maisie's Marriage* at such a moment constituted a strategic intervention in a broader debate, any relationship between the latter and the former pivots as much on discourses surrounding the film as on the content of the film itself. These include, but are by no means confined to, contemporary preoccupations around sexuality, sexual pleasure and contraception. *Maisie's Marriage* is at once produced by these discourses and productive of meanings of its own, meanings which, in a series of complex and at times contradictory operations, recirculate and also transform their originating discourses. The film encounters other practices, too – relations of power through which in specific ways at a particular conjuncture it becomes constituted as a cultural product of a certain kind. Predominant among these are practices of what might be termed the cinematic institution, and within these, more specifically, of film censorship.

Significant in the passage of *Maisie's Marriage* through these apparatuses and practices is the film's association with the name of Marie Stopes. Stopes is credited as writer of the story, though the scenario was actually written by her credited co-writer, Walter Summers, with Marie Stopes maintaining the right of final approval of script and control over the contents of intertitles.[2] The question of precisely who wrote what is beside the point here, though, for the involvement of Marie Stopes in this production far exceeds any conventional understandings of the notion of authorship.

In 1923, the name of Marie Stopes was a byword: her book *Married Love* (subtitled 'a new contribution to the solution of sex difficulties') had been an enormous success from its first publication in March 1918. By the end of that year, in fact, it was already in its sixth reprint. In November 1918, in response to demand by readers of *Married Love*, Stopes published another best-seller, *Wise Parenthood*, a short treatise on birth control (of which there had been only brief discussion in *Married Love*) which included recommendations on methods of contraception. These successes were followed in 1920 by *Radiant Motherhood*, in part advice manual for first-time parents, in part eugenic tract. Marie Stopes's constituency was at first confined largely to the book-buying public – to the middle classes, that is – though within a few years her ideas began to gain much wider circulation.

Marie Stopes's growing fame was perhaps due as much to notoriety – her books were looked on in some influential quarters as nothing less than scandalous, even obscene, and in some countries were banned – as to the social needs addressed by her work. But her writings certainly provoked huge public response, much of which revealed hitherto untapped depths of ignorance, fear, sexual frustration and conjugal misery.[3] At the same time, since they could lay claim to a certain scientific respectability and were endorsed by various eminent medical practitioners, Stopes's ideas could not be dismissed entirely as the outpourings of a crank. The combination of scientificity with sexual subject matter, moral conservatism and romantic appeal guaranteed extensive publicity and a degree of acceptability – as well as controversy – for her work.[4]

In 1923, Marie Stopes's already high public profile was raised several notches when the trial opened in February in a libel suit which she had brought against a Catholic doctor, Halliday Sutherland, who had made some uncomplimentary remarks about birth control in general and Marie Stopes in particular in one of his books. During the nine-day trial other issues were raised, notably the alleged obscenity of *Married Love*. The trial attracted a great deal of publicity, and was reported in all the popular newspapers. On an unclear jury decision, the judge finally ruled in favour of Sutherland, a verdict which produced yet more furore, as well as a good deal of sympathy for the loser. The judgment was taken to appeal, and reversed on 20 July. (The verdict did eventually go against Stopes, however: in November 1924, the Lords ruled four to one in favour of Sutherland.)[5]

During the first half of 1923, then, Marie Stopes and her books were much in the public eye. Controversy raged and sales boomed throughout the year: of *Married Love* alone the number of copies sold leapt from 241,000 to 406,000 between March and December.[6] In the period between the February verdict and the July appeal in the Sutherland case, Stopes made her first – and, as it turned out, her last – foray into fiction cinema as a vehicle for her ideas. *Maisie's Marriage* was produced by Samuelson's, a British company with a reputation for quality films. The film's original title was *Married Love*, but despite its celebration of marital harmony it was in no sense a cinematic version of the book: it made no pretence at being either a scientific treatise or a manual of advice, but was in fact a work of fiction – a 'fast-moving popular melodrama' not very different from the fare on offer in commercial cinemas at the time. Stopes was later to claim that the idea of calling the film *Married Love* had not been hers; whether or not this is so, its producers were evidently well aware of the publicity value attaching to that particular title. The film was made in just two weeks – in an effort, perhaps, to seize the crest of the Sutherland trial publicity wave. It was shown to the trade on 11 May, and scheduled for a June release.

Married Love was well-received by at least one national newspaper,[7] and the trade press, too, was fairly cordial – an attitude which was to be modified in the light of subsequent events. It was, however, pointed out early on that the title could generate expectations that the film could not fulfil. One reviewer nonetheless concluded that

> Whatever may be the suggestion of the title, the film itself is a straightforward human story of sentimental rather than sexual appeal,

while another noted that 'in spite of its title, the story . . . will appeal to the popular imagination'.[8] But if critics emphasised the appeal of the story as against the 'misleading' character of the title, there was already some unease in the trade about the latter. *Kinematograph Weekly*, a journal which saw itself as representing the more 'respectable' elements of the exhibition arm of the film industry, expressed serious misgivings about the choice of title, saying that this was exactly the sort of thing to bring the trade into disrepute.[9] Exploiting the name of a controversial book was far too crude a piece of gimmickry, it seems, to be tolerated in an industry still aspiring to shed the socially inferior image of a sideshow catering to the most vulgar tastes.

However, before *Married Love* was to find its way into the cinemas of the land, it ran into a rather more formidable obstacle. On the day of its trade show, the film was submitted to the British Board of Film Censors, where it languished for more than a month before being released. The Board took exception to the film straight away, on the grounds that

> there are many scenes and sub-titles which render this film in our opinion unsuitable for exhibition before ordinary audiences; while the title, taken in conjunction with the name of the book and the authoress referred to, suggests propaganda on a subject unsuitable for discussion in a Cinema Theatre.[10]

Films based on 'notorious books' were to prove repeatedly troublesome to the Board during 1923, and there was particular disapproval of the use of titles of publications dealing with topics which were regarded as exceeding the proper social function of cinema – namely, to entertain.[11] The BBFC had evidently seen through the producers' bid to capitalise on the publicity value – and the 'forbidden' connotations – of the title *Married Love*. But if this title suggested that the film dealt with issues 'unsuitable' for the cinema, namely, sex and birth control, was there anything in it which might be held objectionable from the standpoint of British film censors of the early 1920s? The Board's verdict, despite its suggestion that the film contained objectionable scenes and intertitles, must have been that there was really very little, if anything, in its content that could specifically be objected to. And yet they were very reluctant to grant it a certificate.

In this atmosphere of uncertainty, the BBFC took the unusual step of asking the Home Office for guidance. On 18 May, a week after the film had been submitted for censorship, officials from the Home Office called at the Board's premises to view *Married Love*.[12] In the interim there had been a protest from Marie Stopes to the BBFC president, T. P. O'Connor (who was a Catholic – a fact which was to figure large in Stopes's assessment of events), and a discussion between O'Connor and the film's producers.[13] Presumably, no agreement had been reached, and O'Connor told the Home Office that he was inclined to refuse to pass the film. The Home Office representatives, however, took a slightly less negative view about the film's content ('there is nothing of an objectionable nature that could not be easily removed by the censor's pruning knife'), though they did agree that there were problems about its title. Their private opinion, nevertheless, was that 'a Birth control-Marie Stopes-propaganda film ought not to appear with a censor's certificate if this could be avoided' –[14] acknowledgment that the trouble was not the actual film, but its association with a 'notorious' public figure and a topic that was at once taboo and controversial.

In other circumstances, perhaps, *Married Love* might at this point, with the collusion of the Home Office and the Board of Censors, have been quietly suppressed. But it was not, for several reasons. Because neither the BBFC nor the Home Office possessed legal powers to censor films, they could strictly speaking do no more than advise the bodies which did hold such powers, namely, the local cinema licensing authorities. Prominent among these was the London County Council, which since the BBFC's inauguration a decade earlier had assumed the role of pacesetter for censorship practices up and down the country. The Board of Censors was eager to maintain good relations with the LCC, which was represented at the 18 May meeting. However, on the question of *Married Love*, the Council disagreed with the BBFC, finding it unobjectionable. This difference of opinion provoked anxieties at the Home Office about possible discord between the BBFC and local cinema licensing authorities, or indeed between the various authorities themselves, as to the film's censorability. For if either of these things were to come about, the national uniformity in film censorship practices, which the Home Office had been striving for a number of years to bring about, and which it now felt was at last in sight, would immediately be undermined.

At stake too was a challenge to the BBFC's hitherto rather shaky authority and credibility. After ten years of indecision and struggle, it was hoped within the government that the Board's tenuous legal position was about to achieve at least conventional consolidation, and that local authorities would soon automatically look to the BBFC for advice on the censorship and certification of films. To this end, the Home Office was preparing a new set of recommended model conditions for cinema licences: these were to include, for the first time and after some legal struggles, a provision that no films without the BBFC's certificate could be exhibited without the express consent of the licensing authority (see chapter 2). When the Home Office was called in to give advice on *Married Love*, these new conditions were in the process of being drafted: they eventually formed the basis of a circular sent to local authorities on 6 July.[15] In this delicately-balanced situation, any upset in relations between the parties involved – Home Office, Board of Censors, local authorities – brought on by the *Married Love* affair was clearly to be avoided. 'I am afraid', said the government official reporting on the 18 May meeting, 'that the film is bound to cause controversy but it is a pity it has come at a time when we were hoping to secure greater uniformity.'[16]

By 1923, the BBFC, over the ten chequered years of its existence, had evolved a set of censorship procedures, including some rules or guidelines as to the sorts of subjects which were acceptable in films destined for commercial exhibition, and as to what was, in the Board's term, 'prohibitive'.[17] 'Controversy' was regarded with automatic suspicion, and this covered not only the sphere of public order – strikes, revolutions, any treatment of 'politics' – but also all matters of 'public morality', which included not only sex *per se* but related topics such as divorce, abortion, contraception and venereal disease. For several years, 'propaganda' films on these topics had automatically been refused certificates (see chapter 4).

Despite its similarity in subject matter to the film discussed in chapter 3, *Where Are My Children*, *Married Love* was constructed through censorship as a very different object. In particular, unlike *Where Are My Children*, it was never really regarded as a 'propagandist' film: it was taken more or less without question as inhabiting the space of commercial/entertainment cinema. Consequently, it could not be treated as belonging to an already excluded category of films. There was little in it, either, that the Board of Censors could call 'prohibitive'. Nevertheless, it was seen as potentially controversial – a 'problem' to be handled with the utmost care.

Married Love remained at the BBFC for several weeks while the Censors were trying to arrive at a decision about it. In response to protests at the continuing delay, the Board wrote to the producers saying the film had been viewed four times and that 'careful and prolonged consideration' was still required.[18] But finally on 7 June a list of alterations was agreed between the two parties. After all the delay, the changes demanded by the Censor were few and on the whole minor in nature, the most significant being that the film's title should be changed to *Maisie's Marriage*, and that posters and other promotional material were not to say that it was based on Marie Stopes's book *Married Love*. Apart from this, eight intertitles were objected to, though only one of these was to be deleted; for the rest, amendments were requested.[19] These changes having been agreed, the BBFC passed the film 'A' (for 'public' exhibition – recommending exhibition to adults-only audiences). Perhaps as a trade-off for the certificate, the London County Council lent the weight of its support to the BBFC's demands for changes, and checked a number of attempts within its area to show the film in uncensored form, or to advertise it 'misleadingly'.[20] The Board expressed the hope that other licensing authorities would be equally vigilant.[21]

This expectation, however, was to prove vain. Within a fortnight of the agreement, it had been brought to the BBFC's attention that the producers of *Maisie's Marriage* had not in fact made all the changes asked for, that uncensored prints of the film were in circulation, and that in many places the name of Marie Stopes was being used in promotion in breach of the spirit of the understanding between the Board and the film's producers. Some exhibitors were apparently advertising the film as '*Maisie's Marriage* – a story of married love written by Dr Marie Stopes'. Worse still, there were reports that the film had been judged unobjectionable by some local authorities, which were presumably permitting exhibition of the uncut version in their areas.[22] 'Respectable' elements of the film trade, having already given their backing to the BBFC in the matter of the film's censorship, expressed their disapproval of exhibitors who were flouting the censors.[23]

These reports were not entirely without foundation. Marie Stopes later conducted an informal survey of local authorities, discovering that a

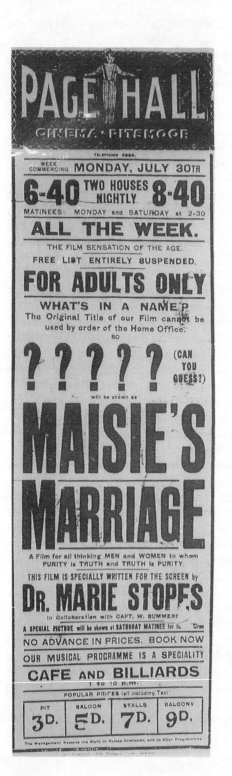

Fig. 10 A Sheffield cinema
defies the Censors: poster
announcing *Maisie's Marriage*

number of them had indeed permitted the exhibition of *Maisie's Marriage* in uncensored form. She was angry about not having been consulted about changes made to the film, whose distributor afterwards claimed that before it was put into circulation, all of the cuts had in fact been restored.[24] In the version of the film discussed here some, but not all, of the changes demanded by the BBFC have been made. It is likely in fact that several different versions were in circulation.

Whatever the case, the Home Office was convinced that a 'fraudulent and impudent evasion'[25] had indeed taken place, and was moved to take the unprecedented step of intervening directly at local level in the censorship of a film. On 30 June, a confidential administrative circular was issued to local licensing authorities in England and Wales, endorsing the BBFC's and the LCC's actions with regard to *Maisie's Marriage*, and expressing the hope that local authorities would 'only allow the revised form of the film to be exhibited under the conditions agreed to by the publishers'.[26] But even this remarkable excursion into state censorship failed to produce the desired effect.[27]

Furthermore, the film's producers managed to find out about the Home Office's 'confidential' circular, and within three weeks of its issue, Marie Stopes had threatened the Home Office with legal action and discussed the matter with the Home Secretary, who responded in somewhat conciliatory manner by assuring her that there had never been any intention that her name should be excluded from the film or from advertisements for it. Nevertheless, while admitting that the Censor's ruling had no status in law, the Home Office refused to climb down to the extent of withdrawing the 30 June circular.[28] Just a few days later, in a renewed wave of publicity, the judgment on appeal in the Stopes-Sutherland libel case was handed down. This coincidence of events ensured the success of *Maisie's Marriage*.[29] Censorship had produced the very opposite effect to that which had been intended.

Popular cinema and a film with a message

Not ours to preach nor yet to point a moral – yet if, in the unfolding of our story, there is aught that comforts, helps or guides, then are our efforts doubly paid.

So begins *Maisie's Marriage*, [30] at once disclaiming and confirming its status as a film with a message. After this, the story begins:

The Burrows family live in Slumland but their prototypes dwell in all our cities – wherever our artificial civilisation has planted its weeds where the struggle for existence is hard and ruthless and the narrow dogma of our disciplined beliefs turn life and the joys of living into meaningless phrases.

The 'Slumland' setting is a concession to the BBFC which objected to the geographical specificity of the original Camberwell. Maisie's family, the Burrowses, are characterised as representing a particular social group, one whose misery is signalled in the scene of poverty, overcrowding and familial discord which follows the opening intertitle: mother overworked and weary, children quarrelsome, babies snivelling, father drunk and violent. Next we are introduced to Maisie, the film's heroine and eldest of the ten Burrows children, at work as a waitress: smart, pretty, polite and smiling, yet capable of handling with firmness and determination customers' sexual advances. If the other Burrowses are specimens of the 'weeds' referred to in the introduction, their ill-kempt garden has somehow produced a perfect rose in Maisie.

What is already implicit in the contrasting characterisations and locations of these first two scenes – that Maisie does not really belong with her family – is rapidly confirmed in the story that follows. The agency of the inevitable separation between Maisie and the rest of the Burrowses comes in the character of Dick Reading, a fireman stationed opposite Maisie's place of work, an only child who enjoys an affectionate relationship with his mother. The young pair are brought together by Dick's dog, and their encounter inspires in Maisie both intimations of erotic pleasure ('dim tremulous thoughts of waking womanhood') and fear of what yielding to such impulses will bring ('It's drudgery and then it will be children, children, and we can't afford to clothe and keep them'). Unwilling to face the prospect of becoming like her cowed and wornout mother, Maisie refuses Dick's offer of marriage, even though she loves him. But Maisie's parting from her sweetheart also brings about her separation from her family: her brutish father, overhearing her telling Dick 'I'm afraid you'd be like my father in a few years', throws her out for her ingratitude:

> 'Now listen ter me, girl – if yer father's roof ain't good enough ter shelter yer – yer'd better pack yer fings and clear – and good riddance to yer.'

Maisie, like many another romantic heroine, is all alone in a world which turns out to be full of pitfalls for an attractive and sexually innocent young woman. On her first night away from home, she falls into the company of prostitutes and narrowly avoids losing her virtue to a man whose wife's frigidity has forced him to seek solace elsewhere. Fortunately, he turns out to be a gentleman and Maisie escapes intact, only to be frightened out of her wits ('Forms that lurk in every shadow – Faces that leer at every turn') merely by finding herself where no decent girl ought to be – out alone on the streets. Desperate, she tries to commit suicide by jumping off a bridge, but is saved from drowning by Paul Sterling, a successful and comfortably-off writer whose wife immediately takes pity on Maisie and offers to take her home. But Maisie's troubles are far from over: her suicide attempt brings her to court, where she is sentenced to two months' imprisonment.

Through a series of lacks – of a proper family life, of a man, and (most important of all) of a particular type of knowledge – Maisie is exposed to a whole range of perils. It is not merely that, in common with many an *ingénue* heroine of silent cinema, Maisie's virtue is constantly at risk: so too are her liberty and even her life. But the conventions of the narrative genre to which this story belongs – the popular romance – as well as the imperatives of the vehicle of its telling – popular cinema – demand a happy ending. For this to be possible, Maisie's lacks must be liquidated and Maisie herself brought from danger to safety.[31]

The first lack – of a family – is in some measure dealt with by the intervention of the Sterlings, who take Maisie into service as a maid when she is released from prison. The Sterling family is all that the Burrowses are not: small, financially secure, and happily ensconced in a delightful home with a huge garden. The Sterlings have three charming and adored children, whose antics awake in Maisie 'the longing that has dwelt unaltered through the ages in every woman's heart'. But it is clear that the Sterlings cannot provide Maisie with the 'proper' family she lacks. Aside from a not inconsiderable difference of class, Maisie can never be a 'real' mother to the Sterlings children, nor even, as it turns out, can she be an adequate mother-substitute: they already have a nanny, and when Maisie is eventually given sole charge of them, disaster strikes – the house catches fire. Maisie may long for happiness of the kind the Sterlings enjoy, but she can never attain it by becoming part of that family. Instead she must deal with the lack of a proper family by making her own, which in the world of the popular romance can mean only one thing – the liquidation of another of the narrative's lacks, Maisie's of a man. Maisie must marry.

And that, of course, is exactly how the story – 'like all true fairy tales', in the words of the film's closing title – ends. But what of the problem that separated Maisie from both her sweetheart and her family of origin in the first place, her fear of the consequences of marriage? Here again the agency of the Sterlings – or more precisely that of Mrs Sterling – is crucial. For it is Mrs Sterling who explains that what Maisie most fears is not after all inevitable:

1 IT: 'I will tell you a story, dear, a parable. There were two men each owning a garden of roses, but the trees of the first grew wild and untended'
2 MCU two-shot Maisie and Mrs Sterling talking.
  FADE.
3 MS a sickly-looking rose bush.

Fig. 11 *Maisie's Marriage*: Mrs Sterling and her children – the perfect family Maisie lacks

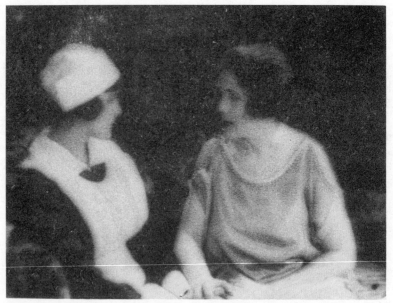

Fig. 12 *Maisie's Marriage*: the parable of the roses – 'I will tell you a story, dear'

4 IT: 'But though the blossoms grew heavy on the branches, they were meagre and colourless'
5 MCU unhealthy-looking roses. FADE.
6 As shot 2.
7 IT: 'But the other was wiser – armed with knowledge he pruned his trees carefully'
8 As shot 6.
9 MCU hands pruning a rose.
10 IT: 'each bud was cared for and nurtured, and though his roses were fewer – each bud had turned into a perfect flower'
11 MS some perfect roses. DISSOLVE.
12 CU one perfect rose. DISSOLVE into face of baby. FADE.

Maisie, the rose among the weeds, now has it within her power not only to produce perfect roses of her own, but also to secure lasting conjugal bliss with a true lover. All that remains is for the former sweethearts to be reunited in a dramatic scene in which Maisie is rescued from fire by Dick and his ever-faithful dog. Not only does Maisie get her man, she will – it is implied – also enjoy 'married love' and a planned family.

Maisie's Marriage can be read at a number of levels, though only one approach is strictly necessary to a 'culturally competent' reading of the film. Cultural competence in this context calls for familiarity – shared within a cultural or a subcultural group of readers – with the particular conventions of narration or representation deployed in a text: a reading of *Maisie's Marriage* as a certain kind of story both demands and produces such competence. At this level, *Maisie's Marriage* may be regarded as a commonplace love story, with elements of drama, suspense and action, and with characterisations and narrational strategies typical of the fiction cinema of the period. Among these are a 'woman-in-peril' theme (Maisie endures trials by water and by fire), drama and suspense created through action and cross-cutting (evident notably in the two scenes in which Maisie is rescued), tender love scenes (Dick's proposals of marriage), melodramatic conflict (family rows, Maisie in court standing trial for attempted suicide), sentimentality (Dick's dog, the Sterling children, their kittens), themes of female virtue and male rapacity (two scenes in which Maisie deals with sexual harassment at work, her excursion into London lowlife with the prostitutes); and a 'fairy tale' ending (the wedding of Maisie and Dick in the final scene). All things considered, *Maisie's Marriage* is certainly readable as no more complex than an ordinary popular romance, in which lovers are parted through no fault of their own, and after a series of vicissitudes are reunited and marry.

In this type of story, the narrative pivots on the cause of the lovers' parting. In *Maisie's Marriage*, it is fear – fear not so much of sex itself as of what the heroine sees as its inevitable consequences – which separates

Fig. 13 '... though the blossoms grew heavy on the branches, they were meagre and colourless'

Fig. 14 '... armed with knowledge, he pruned his trees carefully'

Fig. 15 '... and though his roses were fewer – each bud had turned into a perfect flower'

Fig. 16 A 'perfect flower' is like a bonny baby

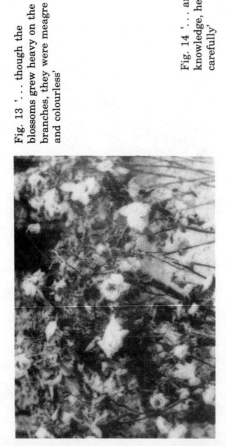

the lovers. A satisfactory resolution of the narrative calls for a dissolution of Maisie's fears about sexual love and marriage, which is brought about by her enlightenment on certain issues. However, it is at exactly the level of questions of sexuality, sexual pleasure, family limitation and marital harmony that the film exceeds its purely narrative enunciation, embodying a discourse that, while taking the narrative as its starting point, also transcends it. This excess constitutes what may be termed the social address of the film, and it is at this level that the 'message' of *Maisie's Marriage* is articulated.

By definition, narrative films with 'messages' adopt positions on, or speak on behalf of, issues which are in some sense external to the individual fiction in question, but which are at the same time dovetailed with it. The merits of such films are commonly judged according to the smoothness with which fiction and 'message' are interwoven, since there is always a risk that the one might dominate the other. If the 'message' dominates, a film can be dismissed as 'mere' propaganda, while if the story is paramount, the 'message' easily becomes submerged; or – and this may simply be another way of saying the same thing – the film may open itself up to a range of different, and potentially conflicting, readings. Given the ascendancy of fictional narrative in cinema and the expectations this generates in audiences, the latter type of 'film with a message' can be rather unstable as a bearer of meaning.

If *Maisie's Marriage* is considered in these terms – for the fictional narrative form had certainly assumed hegemony within the cinematic institution by 1923 – it is clear that the film belongs to the category in which story is paramount. Thus as a film with a message – if not as a romantic narrative – it may be regarded as in some degree 'open', and its social message optional. It might nevertheless be useful to look at the film in terms of how it articulates discourses through which different meanings are produced, in other words – if only because this raises the question of the precise conditions under which particular readings of a film become available.

This is pertinent to the issue of the social message of *Maisie's Marriage*. For in order to read the film as being 'about' birth control, or 'about' sex or sexual pleasure, certain sorts of knowledge must guide its reading: for example, a prior awareness of the existence of Marie Stopes, of the general tenor of her ideas, and perhaps a more direct acquaintance with the contents of books such as *Married Love* and *Wise Parenthood*. The events surrounding the various attempts at suppressing the film would certainly suggest that such knowledge was indeed at stake. All the parties involved in these events agreed that the film's capacity to disseminate ideas, to make money, or to make trouble, lay precisely in its association with the name of Marie Stopes and all that this implied, particularly in the summer of 1923. The conflict was never really about the film's content; it was about the conditions under which it was constructed as a film with a particular message.

What is the nature of this embattled message of *Maisie's Marriage*, then, and how does it engage those discourses which allow the film to be read as bearing a particular message? First of all, the message is not unitary: it incorporates a number of voices, some of which are more insistent than others. Among the most insistent must be the relationship the film sets up, notably in the scenes in the Burrows household, between large families, poverty and unhappy home life. However, to make a connection between these things and a failure to limit fertility calls for a certain amount of knowledge about birth control, for the point is certainly not made explicitly in the film. Second, and related to this, it might be inferred from the ways in which Dick and his mother, and more particularly the Sterlings, are represented, that small families are happy and healthy families. Again, this does not on its own call forth the conclusion that they may be so by intention more than by chance, though this is certainly hinted at in the one intertitle cut from the film at the BBFC's request. In explaining to Dick why she will not marry him, Maisie says: 'Your father died before he did the harm mine's done.'

It is in the sequence in which Mrs Sterling tells Maisie the parable of the rose growers, though, that the film approaches the birth control question most directly. The pruning metaphor, lifted from *Wise Parenthood*,[32] encapsulates Marie Stopes's characteristic combination of eugenic and health/welfare arguments on behalf of birth control. To readers of that book among the film's audience, the reference would be obvious. But the sequence condenses into a few shots a rather specific set of birth control arguments, which would not at the time have been universally endorsed even within the birth control movement itself. These images operate metaphorically, and their meaning is in no measure fixed by the intertitles. On its own, then, the 'parable' remains relatively 'open', though the shot in which a close-up of a rose dissolves into a baby's face does provide the film's least oblique allusion to birth control. The metaphor of pruning is anchored to some extent, then, though significantly not verbally. Contraception must remain unspoken in the text.

A 'social' reading of *Maisie's Marriage* extracts more than simply an endorsement of birth control, however, even if this might be its readiest message. The film is also 'about' sexual pleasure in marriage, which was in fact the central topic of the book *Married Love*. According to Stopes, the control of fertility was a necessary, but by no means sufficient, condition of marital happiness. She advanced the view that sex was a good thing (though only within marriage) and its enjoyment a positive value in itself, essential to conjugal bliss and family contentment. To this end, she exhorted husbands to be sensitive to their wives' sexual needs and desires, and both husbands and wives to perfect their lovemaking techniques.[33]

Nothing of this, of course, is explicit in *Maisie's Marriage*, though to readers of *Married Love* references to Stopes's views on sex would be obvious enough at various points throughout the film.[34]

For Marie Stopes, sexual pleasure in marriage and a frank and open attitude to discussion of sexual matters went hand-in-hand with a happy and loving partnership between husband and wife. The flamboyantly sentimental manner in which this aspect of Stopes's teaching was at times expressed in her writings[35] also has its echoes in the film, where such expression fits well with the generic requirements of the romantic narra-tive. As Mrs Sterling says to Maisie after telling her the parable of the roses:

'Before I married I used to think of my lover – somewhere in the world – searching for me – passing all others by – never resting till we met – and I think this is true, dear.'

To a considerable extent, then, *Maisie's Marriage* is readable as a film with a message only by virtue of its participation in certain discourses on sexuality, sexual pleasure and birth control. It acquires its social address in its engagement with such discourses, especially as they operate in the writings of Marie Stopes. This does not, however, mean that a social reading of the film would have been available only to readers of Stopes's books, simply that prior knowledge of this kind offers ready access to a certain reading of the film. Stopes's name was known to millions who had never read a word she had written; she was a highly controversial figure and her work touched on topics which had the seductive lure of the taboo. Moreover, at the time *Maisie's Marriage* appeared, her court appearances in the Sutherland libel suit had placed her in the forefront of public awareness. If many people did not know precisely what Marie Stopes's ideas were, they certainly knew what they were about: sex and birth control. Whether or not Stopes's name was attached to them, these were burning issues of the day.

It is in this context that the social address of *Maisie's Marriage* is to be understood. To the extent that such an address speaks through the film text, it may be heard in part or in whole, soft and muted, or loud and clear. Indeed, it need not even be heard at all, for the film is perfectly intelligible without it. And yet it was the film's social address that inspired the mobilis-ation of all the apparatuses of censorship, and it is precisely through censorship that the film is constructed as troublesome, as conveying a 'controversial' message. In this sense, censorship did for the film what the film could not have done for itself.

But if *Maisie's Marriage* acquires certain meanings by virtue of discourses in circulation outside the film text itself, these meanings pervade the text at a number of levels. Apart from being readable as popular romance or as a film with a social message, *Maisie's Marriage* can be regarded as dealing also with the problem of *knowledge*. Maisie lacks knowledge of a particular kind, and it is Mrs Sterling who, with her happy family and loving husband, possesses and passes on the knowledge that Maisie lacks. In this respect, *Maisie's Marriage* departs from propaganda films, which typically constitute institutions and practices such as science, medicine, social welfare and the law as repositories and agencies of knowledge. Where, in a propaganda film, knowledge is enunciated by an individual character in the fiction, that character – as noted in the previous chapter – invariably stands in for some institutional source of knowledge. But if the Mrs Sterling character in *Maisie's Marriage* is a stand-in, what exactly is she representing? Women's traditional knowledge of matters emotional, sexual and reproductive? Possibly, but the portrayal of the Sterlings – of Mrs Sterling in particular – suggests otherwise: that Mrs Sterling, independent-minded, happily married purveyor of useful knowledge and good advice, is none other than Marie Stopes herself.

This conclusion acquires added force on examination of the class relations of knowledge proposed by the film. The working class, represented by the Burrowses, Maisie, Dick Reading and his mother, is constructed as either lacking in knowledge, or incapable of articulating knowledge, or both. Yet since the narrative demands that a working-class heroine acquire it, the missing knowledge must be provided from some source or other. Sure enough, it is: a middle-class woman, who is also the employer of its recipient, is that source. Knowledge is imparted, then, not so much in a relation of gender solidarity – a woman passing on female lore to another woman – as through a connection that, for this purpose alone, crosses a social class divide. It is class difference, then, rather than gender solidarity which here provides the condition for the communication of narratively crucial knowledge.

The 'truth' about sexual pleasure, about birth control, about married love, is not universally available in society, nor is it evenly distributed between the different classes. But it can nevertheless be communicated across class barriers by good works – acts of personal kindness, generosity or patronage by the middle class towards the working class. If this sums up Marie Stopes's personal view of her mission to enlighten the working classes in matters sexual and reproductive, it represents only one of several positions in circulation at the time within the birth control movement on the question of the dissemination of knowledge.[36] In this sense, *Maisie's Marriage* adopts, at a certain level, a somewhat partisan stance in its advocacy of birth control – a stance precisely privileging Marie Stopes (or 'Marie Stopes').[37] To the extent that it instates 'Stopes-as-sex-expert' as the authoritative source of knowledge about 'married love', *Maisie's Marriage* also restates the contentions at the forefront of the Stopes-Sutherland libel trial. Could Marie Stopes legitimately represent scientific authority in matters which, shorn of the protective cloak of science, would certainly have been considered 'indecent'? Or was this knowledge sufficiently guaranteed by personal experience, by Stopes's image as a happily-married woman? It is significant that Marie Stopes stood for both these things, and it was perhaps the combination which made her work so controversial.

The trajectory of enunciation of knowledge in *Maisie's Marriage*, however, may enter into conflict with the narrative and cinematic imperatives of the genre to which the film, as popular cinema, belongs. If the romantic narrative requires that lovers be subjected to needless separation in order that they may ultimately be reunited, it also demands that the reader understand more than the unfortunate couple about exactly what it is that has separated them. The reader must be aware that the lovers' parting is unnecessary in order that the pleasure of its poignancy can be fully indulged while the reader remains safe in the knowledge that matters can, and certainly will, be sorted out in the end. In the case of *Maisie's Marriage*, then, generic imperatives would suggest that spectators of the film ought to know what Maisie does not know. But, as has been noted, while in 1923 some audience members might well have been in this position, many undoubtedly were not: this would call for knowledge which was in many respects esoteric at this time.

To the extent that *Maisie's Marriage* addresses a knowing spectator, and to the extent that readers of *Married Love* would be forearmed with the necessary knowledge, the film's address must surely be, in some degree at least, class-specific. Given the social composition of the book-buying public, the film would divide its audience into groups with distinct narrative viewpoints. Spectators who have no more understanding than Dick and Maisie themselves as to what has brought about their separation assume the standpoint of these characters – a 'view with'. On the other hand, spectators with access to such an understanding are in a position to occupy a 'view behind', since they know more than the characters.[38]

What is important here is that the knowledge necessary for the assumption of a narrative 'view behind' cannot be spoken in the film itself: it has to be brought to its reading. There are two main reasons for this. Firstly, the conventions of popular cinema limit the extent to which matters of information can be dealt with in a fiction feature film without its sliding over into the 'propaganda' category. And in any case, overt expressions of the kind of knowledge required in order to guarantee the spectator a 'view behind' would certainly have been 'prohibitive' at this period. In this sense, a 'view behind' is sustained by knowledge prior to the film, for the knowledge around whose absence the film's narrative pivots cannot be articulated within the text itself.

The audience addressed by the film consequently divides – to a considerable extent most probably along class lines – into those who already know and those who do not know but probably 'ought' to. As a piece of popular romantic fiction, *Maisie's Marriage* constructs an audience in the former category; as a 'film with a message', in the latter. And since the film was constituted as censorable almost entirely with regard to its status as a 'message' film, then the problem as regards censorship was precisely that section of the audience that did not know – broadly speaking, the working class.

I have suggested that the excessive censorship activity provoked by *Maisie's Marriage* had a great deal to do with the film's association with the name of Marie Stopes. It is clear that the various parties involved in the processes of censorship were well aware of this; and it is apparent, too, that they were at some level conscious of the film's instability as a carrier of knowledge of certain kinds. The BBFC's most significant demands – that the title *Married Love* not be used and that no suggestion be made in advertising the film that it was based on Marie Stopes's book – show this clearly enough, for they are aimed precisely at inhibiting the availability (especially to that section of the audience that 'did not know') of a 'social' reading of the film. Hence the strongly-expressed irritation of both Censors and Home Office officials, and the unprecedented resort of the latter to direct intervention at local level, when infringements of these prohibitions came to light.

But Marie Stopes's figuration in *Maisie's Marriage* operates at several levels, not all of them susceptible to the operations of censorship. First, and most obviously, Stopes the individual figures as the film's author: in the opening title, she is co-credited, complete with academic qualifications, with its writing:

G. B. Samuelson presents
MAISIE'S MARRIAGE
A Story specially written for the Screen
by
DR MARIE STOPES DSc PhD
in collaboration with
CAPTAIN WALTER SUMMERS

At this level censorship was powerless to intervene, much as those involved might have wished to do so: Marie Stopes, a leading member of the Society of Authors, was in a position to see to it that she kept her writer's credit on the screen at least.[39] As to the film's advertising and promotion, these matters rested ultimately with the film trade, with exhibitors in particular, rather than with either Marie Stopes on the one hand or the British Board of Film Censors on the other.

Second, and more importantly, Marie Stopes – or perhaps rather her writings and other propagandising activities – figures as the locus of that knowledge which makes possible a reading of *Maisie's Marriage* as a film with a certain message. It is at this reading that the operations of censorship were mainly directed. But these efforts at prohibition had unexpected, even contradictory, effects: far from limiting the availability of a 'social' reading of the film, they actually invited such a reading, certainly once the prohibition was made public. Finally, there is one more level at which Marie Stopes – or 'Marie Stopes' – figures in the film: this is the point at which 'Stopes' is constituted as the enunciative source of narratively crucial knowledge. This level is beyond the reach of any institutional procedures of censorship. As the BBFC's rather paltry demands for alterations indicate, there was little in the film that could be regarded, certainly in terms of these procedures, as 'prohibitive'. These minor changes, in combination with the efforts made to circumscribe readings of the film, may be regarded as symptomatic of a certain awareness that its troublesome qualities far exceeded any question of censorable content.

The productivity of censorship

Institutional practices of film censorship are obliged to assume as their object individual films – texts, representations which are in some sense bounded; and yet in any actual instance of censorship there is always more than this at stake. Certainly in the case of *Maisie's Marriage* the content of the film does not provide sufficient explanation either for the excessive censorship activity it provoked, nor for the consequences of that activity, many of which were unforeseeable and some indeed the very opposite of what had been intended. *Maisie's Marriage* became an object of censorship by virtue of its implication, at a specific moment, within certain discourses and power relations, which penetrate the text and yet also exceed it. These include discourses and practices of film censorship; but also involved in the constitution of *Maisie's Marriage* as censorable are on the one hand the operations of the film industry and on the other contemporary debates around sexuality and birth control. Each of these – censorship, the film industry, discourses on sexuality – constructs the film differently, and each is caught up in a struggle over the conditions under which the film was to enter the public domain. Each, too, inscribes different – and sometimes contradictory – power relations.

As a product of the British film industry of the early 1920s, *Maisie's Marriage* may be regarded as an unexceptional piece of commercial fiction cinema, comfortably occupying, both thematically and stylistically, one of the popular film genres of the day – a marketable enough commodity, perhaps, though it had to contend with the firmly established hegemony in Britain of American cinema.[40] For its producers, of course, it had something extra, something that promised to make it a much better box-office proposition than any run-of-the-mill British-made love story was liable to be: it could trade upon the name of Marie Stopes, a name which in 1923 was a byword for the forbidden and alluring topic of sex. In their bid to call the film *Married Love*, its producers hoped to maximise the potential of Stopes's authorship by implying that the film, like the book – or, for that matter, the image of the book in the public mind – was 'about' sex. But this elicited the response from other sections of the film trade that such a patent attempt at deception could only bring the industry into further disrepute. These elements aligned themselves with the British Board of Film Censors to the extent, once the film had been released, of condemning not so much the film itself as the way it was being promoted.

If one of the principal objectives of the BBFC was to avoid controversy, it found a powerful ally in the Home Office; it was perhaps due only to a coincidence of timing that the film was not suppressed. The summer of 1923 was a critical moment for institutional practices of film censorship in Britain. The Board of Censors was on the very threshold of finally attaining the credibility it considered crucial for its survival, and avoidance of open conflict between it and local cinema licensing authorities was felt to be essential. The matter had therefore to be handled with the greatest care. Since at least one powerful local authority found *Maisie's Marriage* unobjectionable, there was no alternative but to certificate the film, and so permit its entry into the public domain as a film suitable – under certain conditions at least – for commercial exhibition.

The routine procedures of film censorship at this period were instrumental in determining the limits of what was and what was not 'suitable' material for commercial cinema screens. If *Maisie's Marriage* could not be faulted either in content or in style, the film's connection with the controversial name of Marie Stopes made it extremely troublesome, all the more so because there was very little in the film itself that could seriously be objected to. If the film was produced as an object of censorship through its implication in contemporary debates around sexuality and birth control, these issues are not explicitly spoken in it. This made it a peculiarly elusive object of censorship. One of the difficulties *Maisie's Marriage* posed *vis-à-vis* film censorship was that it was already a product of other contemporary censorships, notably of the widespread taboo on discussion of sexual matters and the virtual impossibility of obtaining information on birth control. Nevertheless, although the film may be open to a variety of readings, meanings in *Maisie's Marriage* become relatively fixed in the moment of censorship, through which it is constructed precisely as 'controversial'. Film censorship creates censorable films, and a censorable film, once it has entered the public domain, becomes a marketable property exactly because of the lure of forbiddenness conferred by known acts of censorship. In the *Maisie's Marriage* affair, censorship operates not only prohibitively – in the regulation of a public sphere of discussion – but also productively – in the actual creation of such a sphere.

6   Sexuality and the Cinema

Only along these lines – by raising the ideal of marriage, by education for parenthood, and by intervening to prevent degeneracy – can we cope with the demoralization which is sapping the foundations of the national wellbeing.

> Manifesto of the National Council of Public Morals, 1911

Science and the socio-sexual

If the films discussed in the last three chapters called forth the acts of censorship directed at them, this was not so much because they were held to be 'indecent' or 'obscene' as because they were regarded as 'controversial'. This, however, begs the question of how controversiality figures in the instances of censorship examined in this inquiry, and also, more generally, how controversiality may be produced as an attribute of representations, an attribute which sanctions certain gestures of censorship.

The question of the controversial quality of certain representations acquires a special inflection *vis-à-vis* cinema as an institution and as a mode of representation, as well as in relation to the specific cases of film censorship examined here. How, it may be asked, does a film or a group of films come to be constituted as censorable? The case histories highlight both the specificity and also the variety and complexity of discourses and power relations involved in such processes. But while any one instance of censorship will embody a unique combination of discourses and power relations, certain general points do seem to emerge from these cases. They arise, of course, after the fact: no 'macro-historical masterplan'[1] is being assumed here.

One such generalisation is that the distinctive relations of power which come to light in each of the case histories are all implicated in discourses around the body and its sexuality, in the broadest sense of both terms. These discourses are instrumental in turn in producing, at particular historical moments, certain forms of knowledge: namely, knowledges which aspire to order the domain of the sexual as it participates in and is contained by the social, and which constitute the body and its sexuality as essentially social processes. I shall term this discursive field the socio-sexual. During the first two decades of this century, certain areas of knowledge competed with each other in the production and circulation of constructs of the socio-sexual. This was not simply a question of the production and dissemination of knowledges, however: their 'application' in the cause of constituting and regulating their objects is also involved.

At issue here, therefore, is the ordering of objects of knowledge, where certain knowledges produce the socio-sexual as an arena of intervention. Power is exercised in the production and deployment of discourses on sexuality, specifically of knowledge about the socio-sexual. But in specific instances of the sort considered in the case histories, such processes are more complex than might be suggested by abstract statements concerning the relationship between knowledge and power. For each of these instances embodies different understandings of both the social and the socio-sexual – and conflicting views about, and strategies for, the perfectibility of these objects. Cinema at this period is actively involved in the deployment of, and indeed in the competition between, various knowledges as they constitute society and the socio-sexual as spheres of intervention and regulation. Specifically, the operations brought to light in the three case histories constitute a series of exchanges, both between religious and 'scientific' discourses, and, more significantly, between different scientific discourses, on the socio-sexual.

In the latter case, during the period under consideration in this inquiry science and sexuality encountered one another in the disciplines of eugenics and sexology. In the earlier part of this period the science of eugenics enjoyed unrivalled pre-eminence as a discipline concerned with certain aspects of human sexuality. As a body of knowledge directed at both measuring and improving the physical and intellectual quality of the population, eugenics concerned itself with questions around reproduction and fertility. Aspiring to scientific authority for their work, eugenists gathered information on fertility; cross-correlated it with variables such as social class, physical and mental health, and environmental conditions; and produced quantitative data on the social-psychological determinants of human fertility. Eugenics, besides being a forerunner of quantitative sociology, also gave birth to what was to become a pervasive and highly authoritative strategy of normalisation, intelligence testing.[2]

If, however, in its quest for scientificity, eugenics aimed to produce 'hard' data on human fertility and its determinants, it made no claim to be a 'pure' science: the substantive findings of eugenic inquiry, in combination with its aspiration to scientificity, gave rise to the characteristically eugenic doctrine that the quality of the population was capable of improvement. Views among eugenists as to the most effective means of going about this task differed somewhat, however. While some favoured a 'negative' eugenics – advocating the discouragement of breeding by the 'unfit', others proposed a 'positive' approach, whereby the most eugenically 'fit' members of the population were to be encouraged to be more fertile.[3]

But whatever their internal differences, the social policies of eugenists were invariably actuated by a broadly demographic set of concerns. From a purely eugenic standpoint, if, say, the health and welfare of individuals and families were regarded as important, this was because these benefits would contribute to the general well-being of 'the race'. Eugenics, in taking as its object entire populations, draws upon and amalgamates a particular set of knowledges – medical science, biological science, social science. Each of these knowledges constructs a specific domain of the socio-sexual as an object not only of investigation and scrutiny, but also of regulation.

While eugenics was at the height of its intellectual currency, another corpus of knowledge relating to the body and its sexuality was in process of formation. Sexology – which initially enjoyed rather less public acceptability than eugenics – also constituted itself as a science, but with an object distinct from that of eugenics: human sexual behaviour and the relations between the sexes. If sexology's object of inquiry differed from that of eugenics, so also did its methods. Sexology aimed not only to record and classify human sexual behaviour in all its variability, but also to set forth the laws which governed it. But to the extent that this project – in its latter aspect, certainly – called for some consideration of the place of sex and sexuality in society, sexology, in common with eugenics, was implicated in the discursive production of a domain of the social. Society, however, is conceptualised rather differently in each case. For sexology, society was a system operating according to a set of laws, discoverable at a general level by means of observing particular social behaviours. If sexuality was a variant of social behaviour, then its 'scientific' study was to be regarded as a constituent of that broader science of society, sociology.[4]

The rise of the discipline of sexology as a scientific discourse of the socio-sexual produced diverse and at times contradictory consequences. It has been argued, for example, that sexology's claim to scientificity has privileged certain views about the nature of sexuality: for example, that sexuality is a force of nature, governed by immutable urges and instinctive forces.[5] At the same time, however, such a view conflicts with the sociologising imperative of a discipline which, in highlighting the cultural variability of sexual behaviour, often aligned itself with 'progressive' causes of sexual enlightenment and social reform. Thus whereas sexology might well have been instrumental, say, in constructing categories of 'normal' as opposed to 'abnormal' sexuality, it also claimed a vanguard position in the struggle against repressive, 'old-fashioned' ideas about sex.

If these two tendencies within sexology were contradictory, their conjunction nevertheless produced a distinctive and significant strategy of normalisation: sex education in general, and more particularly advice and guidance on sexual matters delivered by 'experts' to the general public. In a somewhat transformed state, some of the ideas of the sexologists gained currency in a body of writings – beginning in the 1910s and achieving wider circulation during the 1920s – advancing, among other things, the novel notion that sexual harmony between husband and wife was a cornerstone of happy marriage. Published in 1918, Marie Stopes's *Married Love* was among the best known of many books informed by the arguments of the sexologists and directed at the promotion of sexual pleasure as a good thing in itself, whilst simultaneously circumscribing its objects and the contexts within which it might properly be sought.[6]

Sexology, like eugenics, concerns itself with the socio-sexual. Both aspire, too, to sanction their project of producing knowledge about, of constituting the field of, the socio-sexual by laying claim to a certain scientificity. And both seek to deploy their respective knowledges in the cause of social reform, so that reform becomes a matter of applying scientific knowledge rather than, say, an expression of religious, moral or philanthropic principles. However, the socio-sexual is constituted rather differently by eugenics and by sexology, as are the nature of social reforms envisaged and the means advocated for bringing them about.

Most importantly, perhaps, while the target of eugenic reform was the population as a whole, the enlightenment on sexual questions promised in popular versions of sexology was directed not at 'the race' but at married couples and families. In practice, however, these objectives were not mutually exclusive: as many of the 'sex experts' of the 1920s argued, a 'eugenic' marriage, in which births were planned and fertility controlled, had a better chance of being a happy union than one in which such matters were left to chance. Nevertheless, this general shift of emphasis away from the population towards the wellbeing of the family and the married couple (if not yet to the individual) must be regarded as significant, certainly as regards the concerns of the present inquiry.

In their relations with the apparatuses through which they became constituted as objects of censorship, the films looked at in the three case histories are caught up in a number of ways in this exchange between eugenics and sexology. VD propaganda films, for instance, are marked by a specific eugenic conern: anxiety about the decline of the race as a consequence of the spread of syphilis, a highly contagious and at the time a virtually incurable disease, often contracted sexually but capable also of being passed on to children and other 'innocent' victims. A film like *Where Are My Children*, on the other hand, can be read as articulating a slightly different eugenic preoccupation: fears that the best elements of the population were at risk of being swamped by the prolifically breeding cohorts of the 'unfit' – the lumpenproletariat and the 'feeble-minded'.

Maisie's Marriage, too, can be understood as bearing a eugenic message: the misery of the Burrows family and the depravity of certain of its members would certainly justify such a reading, while the Sterlings' marriage is clearly a eugenic union. In this film, though, a 'hard' eugenic concern with the state of the race is softened to the extent that the fecundity of the Burrowses is proposed as the cause, rather than the effect, of their degeneracy, and the happiness of the Sterlings as a *family* is stressed. At the same time, while this film's stance on eugenics may be seen as positive, even as progressive, there is a sense in which *Maisie's Marriage* is not primarily 'about' eugenics at all. The trajectory of the film's narrative forces it in the direction, precisely, of Maisie's *marriage*. The story's central concern, though, is not merely matrimony, but also marital happiness in a world in which large, unplanned families militate against such a state. The pivotal role accorded in this film to a certain type of knowledge, and to the method by which it is communicated to the heroine, suggest a sexological rather than a eugenic impulse in *Maisie's Marriage*.

But if the films dealt with in this inquiry might be readable as 'speaking' eugenics, or as 'speaking' sexology, this is not to suggest that they simply reproduce or reflect discourses already in circulation outside them. First of all, given that film texts are actively instrumental in the production of such discourses, no fixed and unproblematic boundary can be drawn between the textual and the extratextual. Second, in their implication within, and articulation of, debates around eugenics and sexology, the films operate in a complex and often contradictory manner. For example, the various readings of *Where Are My Children* – a film which was constituted differently in relation to the eugenics question in Britain as against the USA – indicate that meanings immediately available from what appears to be a single and unitary text may vary according to circumstance. In its country of origin, *Where Are My Children* was not seen as being solely, or even at all, 'about' eugenics. In Britain, on the other hand, it was immediately slotted into current preoccupations about the falling birth rate and the decline in the quality of the population. This difference, which had to do largely with the conditions surrounding the film's reception in each country, had important repercussions. In Britain especially, the film's appropriation for eugenics, in combination with emergent conceptualisations of cinema and its proper social function, rendered it highly censorable.

But if a 'eugenic' reading of *Where Are My Children* effectively obliterated the film as a piece of popular fiction, the specificity of cinema – as a mode of representation, as a set of relations between films and their consumers, and as an industry devoted to the production and circulation of a particular type of commodity – must also be taken into consideration in considering the relationship between film texts and discourses which also circulate outside them. Fiction cinema has its own imperatives, and in certain circumstances these may impede, even undercut, the logic of discourses with which it comes into contact – and indeed vice versa. Processes of discursive productivity, interchange and transformation are at work here.

For example, conventions of fiction cinema arguably obstruct rather than facilitate the expression of eugenic or sexological ideas. Cinematic narrative cannot be regarded as a neutral vehicle through which ideas which pre-exist films are conveyed through films. On the contrary, as each of the case histories demonstrates, the characteristic privileging of the individual and the dramatic in fiction cinema through its emphasis on character and action specifies, even at moments occludes, issues which go beyond the narrative. Film, in other words, deals with such matters in its own way, at times with unexpected consequences. If – at a particular period – cinema, and specifically fiction cinema, was taken up as a vehicle for disseminating 'scientific' knowledge of various kinds, science certainly did not have things all its own way. As a signifying system, fiction cinema might not have barred the way to science, but it seems to have opened up only those entrances it deemed, in terms of its own conventions, appropriate.

Social hygiene, social purity and social science

The courtship, successful or otherwise, of cinema by science at a certain historical moment may be seen as a bid to advance the epistemological claims of science against those of religion. Eugenics and sexology both constituted themselves as sciences, and both were devoted to a specific approach to the production of knowledge and to the mobilisation of that knowledge in the cause of social reform. If they differed as to their objects of knowledge and objectives of reform, they nevertheless inhabited a similar world of epistemology and value. Both eugenists and sexologists adopted the term 'social hygiene' to characterise their approach to social reform: such a label had the merit of imbuing their activities with overtones of scientificity, while stripping them of the philanthropic and moralising (in short, the 'unscientific') connotations of earlier conceptualisations of social reform.

The struggle between religion and science overarches the exchange, within the latter's sphere, between tenets and programmes of eugenics and sexology: the implicit distinction between social hygiene and social reform may be read as symptomatic of a rivalry between religious and scientific world views. This rivalry was embodied in several contemporary institutions and practices, notable among them being public health. The earliest years of this century saw a renewed interest in public health issues, fuelled largely by a number of scientific 'advances', notably the isolation of the bacilli of certain diseases. These developments had repercussions for the ways in which the highly socially visible disorders of tuberculosis and syphilis were – in all senses of the word – treated. (The syphilis spirochaete, for example, was isolated in 1905, and salvarsan – the earliest cure for the disease known to science – was formulated in 1910.)[7] Although the preoccupations of the social hygiene movement were not the same as those of public health, they shared substantial areas of interest, since both projects were informed by the scientific attitude.

Writing in 1912, the sexologist Havelock Ellis stated that social hygiene is 'a development, and even a transformation, of what was formerly known as Social Reform'.[8] Social hygiene was an advance on social reform, continued Ellis, because it was directed at the prevention of social evils by attacking them at source, an objective made possible by advances in the sciences, particularly in the biological sciences. Ellis's prescriptions for the tasks of social hygiene are grounded not in biology, though, but rather in the sciences of the socio-sexual: eugenics to deal with the problems of the falling birth rate and feminism's deleterious effects upon maternity, sexology to promote sexual instruction for children and to inform the legal regulation of certain sexual behaviours, and a combination of the two to handle the question of 'married love'. The domain of social hygiene, then, is exactly the socio-sexual, which is regarded as an area to be discovered, described, mapped, understood, and finally reformed with the assistance of science. Science, in this view, offered a superior approach to the betterment of society because it was diagnostic: it could predict, and therefore it could also prevent.

The contention that social reform, unlike social hygiene, is an activity that comes into play only after the event, that it deals with the symptoms rather than the causes of social ills, may be seen as a blow struck in a larger battle being waged at this period between the claims of science and those of God in the quest for knowledge and understanding of the world. For God, in these years, was still far from dead: in the arena of social reform, certainly, a religious world view did not merely survive, but flourished in discourses of social purity and public morality. The social purity movement rose to public prominence after the mid-nineteenth century, on a wave of moral indignation about social evils such as prostitution, promiscuity, sexual exploitation and the sexual double standard. With its predominantly moralising impetus, social purity was active, if not always directly and unproblematically so, in several arenas of social reform.[9]

The social purity movement, then, shared with social hygiene the constitution of a socio-sexual sphere as an object of reform. However, rather different understandings of the socio-sexual are at stake in each case. For social purity, the importation of sexuality into the realm of the social rendered the former subject to strategies of surveillance and regulation governed by notions of morality. Morality was regarded as a social, or a public, matter, while specific moral codes were usually seen as in the final instance God-given. Morality, in this view, was no private matter: it inhabited the sphere of the socio-sexual precisely as *public* morality.

This is not, however, to suggest that the battle between science and God, between secularly and religiously grounded knowledges and strategies of reform in the area of the socio-sexual, was waged on terrain neatly divided between two distinct and readily identifiable antagonistic forces. The situation was rather more complex than this, for the period is marked, discursively, by a remarkable degree of interpenetration of religious and scientific world views and associated apparatuses and practices. It is symptomatic and quite characteristic of the time, for example, that a social purity organisation like the National Council of Public Morals should embrace both science and God in its objective of working towards 'the regeneration of the race – spiritual, moral and physical'. This statement of aim manages to combine a eugenically-inspired social hygienist concern about the physical quality of the population with a religiously-based construct of morality as a public sphere of regulation.

Within the terms of such a 'hybrid' discourse, a cinema harnessed to the aspirations of moral reform becomes feasible, and capable at the same time of legitimation in terms of claims to scientificity: hence the sponsorship or promotion of certain films by social purity and/or social hygiene organisations – *Where Are My Children* by the NCPM, for example, and *The End of the Road* by the National Council for Combating Venereal Disease. In specific instances, it is often difficult to assess the degree to which the claims of religion outweigh those of science, or vice versa, for they appear very much interrelated. It is characteristic, for example, that at the launch of *Where Are My Children*, both interests were represented – in the figures respectively of the Bishop of Birmingham, President of the NCPM, and of C. W. Saleeby, sociologist and noted populariser of eugenic ideas. The National Council and bodies like it were usually supported by public figures standing for an extremely wide range of scientific, political and religious interests and shades of opinion.[10] Different knowledges also co-exist within many of the films under consideration in this inquiry. In particular, the VD propaganda genre is marked by a medico-moral discourse in which cure (wrought by science) and salvation (wrought by God) are conflated: in these films, both are typically constituted, in narrative terms, as necessary to the restoration of the integrity of a character who has fallen prey to a sexually transmitted disease.

The imbrication of scientific and religious discourses during this period suggests that their struggle for epistemological ascendancy was intense. The religious world view was evidently very much alive in the fields of social purity and public morality, and quite capable of putting up a fight against the claims of science, even though in most areas of social reform science – at the service not only of voluntary agencies of reform but of the state as well – would in one guise or another eventually win the day. So, for example, the NCCVD's change of name in 1925 to the British Social Hygiene Council may be seen as symptomatic of a shift, in the deployment of knowledge about the socio-sexual, away from purification of the moral body and towards hygienisation of – precisely rendering physically healthy – the social body.

Such a shift is manifest, too, in a growing tendency among agencies of social reform to appeal to certain types of 'scientific' knowledge in support of their activities. When the NCPM mounted its Cinema Commission of Inquiry in 1916 to look into the 'physical, social, educational and moral influences of the cinema', it was participating in the production of a science of the social – of social science, that is – as an adjunct of social reform. Investigations like this promised to confer credibility on reform programmes precisely because the latter could lay claim to scientific pre-dictiveness, precision and objectivity. The Report of the Cinema Commiss-ion, when published in 1917, was the first piece of work of its kind on cinema to appear in Britain; as such it inaugurated a certain strategy of describing, of knowing about, and thus of constituting, cinema. Cinema, concluded the Report, could indeed be a social problem, particularly in relation to certain audiences – though handled in the right way it could also be a Good Thing.

At a certain conjuncture, then, social science and social hygiene forged an alliance in the struggle for secular hegemony over discourses of social reform. As part of this process, the field of the socio-sexual was mapped with the authoritative and powerful assistance of science, in the teeth of religion's counterclaims for it as a domain of public morality. Out of this conflict emerged new approaches to, and objects of, reform. Among the latter was cinema itself, which took its place alongside other components of a social body increasingly conceptualised in terms of degrees of health or sickness, and seen as subject to regulation by interventions considered likely to be effective in the degree to which they were scientifically-grounded. Science, then – in the guise of social science and social hygiene – aspired to become the principal means of restoring the integrity of the social body. At the same time, though, wherever notions of public morality persisted or prevailed in the sphere of the socio-sexual, society continued to be conceptualised also in terms of religiously-based discourses on the body and its sexuality. In such circumstances, both sexual morality and the sexual body became matters of pressing social concern.

The instrumentality of corruption

In a particular set of historical circumstances, then, the sexual body and the social body became assimilated to one another. The case of VD propa-ganda films illustrates how, at a certain moment, the perceived health of the sexual body came to stand in for the integrity – the fitness and the soundness – of an entire society. Such an identification is understandable only in terms of a specific discursive combination of science and religion: on the one hand, discourses of social hygiene which concerned themselves with the health, or lack of it, of society; on the other, discourses of social purity which claimed morality in general, and sexual morality in particular, as matters for public discussion and social regulation.

Any such discursive ensemble must be regarded as conjuncturally specific. In the case once again of discourses surrounding the VD propaganda genre, scientificity made its appearance in a eugenic concern especially prominent in the wake of the moral panic about venereal disease which raged during World War I: it was feared that a rapid spread of VD would inevitably have a deleterious effect on the general physical quality of the population. On the other hand, while – also during the 1910s – a eugenic reading of the film *Where Are My Children* was effectively forced upon it by the conditions of its reception in Britain, the eugenic concern was in this case directed at a decline in birth rate among the middle- and upper-middle classes, a trend which, it was felt, also constituted a threat to the quality of the population.

Underlying such preoccupations with the physical state of a population is an anxiety about its vulnerability to corruption. In this context, corruption must be understood in all its senses: the perversion of something from some original state of purity; taint or contagion; making or becoming morally corrupt; moral deterioration or depravity. A healthy, clean or pure community or society was in danger of being corrupted by disease or decay as long as its 'best stocks' were being swamped by the over-fecund 'unfit'. To the extent that a notion of corruption assumed moral or spiritual, as well as physical, overtones, though, the would-be impartial scientific discourse of eugenics stood at risk of sliding into a social puritanical one of moral judgment. At the same time, however, social hygiene and social purity continued to advance their own distinct remedies for corruption. For the moral reformer, spiritual regeneration was the only corrective, while as an alternative to the purification of the collective soul, science offered the cleansing properties of impartial, secular knowledge. For science, an understanding of how, say, venereal disease is contracted and transmitted was a prerequisite to bringing its racially corruptive effects under control. From a scientific standpoint, it was not so much sin as ignorance – or perhaps rather the 'wrong' sort of knowledge – that corrupted.

In accordance with this view, social hygiene allied itself with the scientific objectives of sex reform in advocating widespread education on sexual matters. The NCCVD, for example, contended that the cause of eliminating venereal diseases would be assisted if young people could receive instruction about the nature and effects of these disorders, and about how they could be avoided and cured. After the VD scare had died down, this organisation – now under a new name – broadened its remit to take in sex education in general, emphasising its commitment to social hygiene. In line with its general policy on education, the NCCVD/BSHC was consistent over many years in supporting 'health propaganda' films. It is on this question of sex education, perhaps, that scientific and religious world views diverged most sharply. Informing young people about sex was regarded in many social purity circles as a moral risk in itself, and even as an incitement to illicit sexual activity. Indeed, in discourses of social purity moral rectitude, sexual innocence, and ignorance often go hand-in-hand.

The fear of corruption that lay at the heart of much eugenic thinking during the earliest years of the twentieth century obviously opened a space for the recursion of a religious world view into 'scientific' knowledge about society, especially when deployed in the service of social reform. Notions about the hygienisation of the race acquired moral and spiritual, as well as mundanely physical, overtones. In the first two decades of this century, and especially during World War I, the discursive conflation of the population's moral with its physical condition coalesced into a set of anxieties about the decline of Britain as a nation. As a consequence, race and nation became constituted as synonymous with one another. The production, promotion and reception of films like *Where Are My Children*, *Damaged Goods* and *The End of the Road* participated in all these discursive processes.

Knowledge, though, is rarely if ever monolithic: eugenics, certainly, incorporated several different positions. After the war ended, eugenic thinking appears to have undergone a shift of emphasis which heralded its eventual decline as the hegemonic scientific discourse of the socio-sexual. From its earliest years, the eugenic movement had always counted among its numbers some who adopted a 'progressive' line on the improvement of the race. Progressive eugenists advocated positive programmes of social reform – including child welfare benefits and better housing – whose end result would be to enhance the overall quality of the population.[11] A concern with the general health, welfare and happiness of the community brings this branch of eugenics close – at the level of policy, certainly – to other reform groups whose overall objectives were actually distinct from those of eugenics. Among these was the birth control movement, which was also supported by sex reformers.[12]

In the 1920s, with the transformation of eugenics and the rise of new scientifically-grounded social hygiene movements, reform began to concern itself less with the state of the race and more with the welfare of families, or the improvement of the life chances of women and/or the working classes. But if these different objectives are founded on dissimilar conceptualisations of the social order, they are not actually mutually exclusive at the level of policy and practice. A film like *Maisie's Marriage*, whose theme sets it apart somewhat from *Where Are My Children* and the VD features, is readable in the light of a movement towards the family and away from the race as a major object of social reform. Nevertheless, this is not to imply that a concern with the family is absent in the earlier films – on the contrary, in fact. In *Damaged Goods*, as I have argued, the hero's transgression is instrumental in, even punished by, the break-up of his family, while a resolution of the film's narrative is dependent upon the family's reconciliation. And in *Where Are My Children*, the tragedy of the Waltons lies exactly in the fact that, doomed to a childless marriage, they will never enjoy a 'real' family life. In fact, in all of the films considered here, regardless of differences of theme and emphasis, a 'proper' family is constituted, if not as a goal towards which the narrative must proceed, then certainly as necessary to the happiness of key characters in the story.

The fact that such a varied group of fiction films shares a preoccupation of one sort or another with the family must be regarded as significant. It suggests, for one thing, that film texts cannot be seen as merely reflecting 'extratextual' processes, such as shifts in discursive constructions of the socio-sexual. While, as I argued in chapter 1, it is misleading to posit any fixed line of demarcation between a film as text and a world of social practice or discourse outside the text – between text and context, in other words – it should be remembered that cinema, as a specific practice of representation, does possess a logic of its own. Thus, for example, if at a certain moment a moral panic about VD mobilised a peculiar combination of eugenic and moralistic thinking in an articulation of anxieties about the decline of the nation, fiction films on the topic had no alternative but to speak these concerns in the 'language' of cinematic narrativity.

Films, then, do not reflect a 'real' world outside the text, nor even – if it is conceptualised as operating prior to its textual formation – any discursively constructed social formation. Cinema is a discursive process in its own right: thus in the present instance, films are themselves actively instrumental in discursive constructions of the socio-sexual. In this process, films – certainly the ones dealt with in this inquiry – tend to privilege the family over the race/nation. At the same time, though, cinema's processes of discursivity cannot be regarded as entirely autonomous of other discourses and practices. Cinema nevertheless does have a momentum of its own. Conventions of cinematic narrativity will privilege individual characters, their actions and their relations with other characters over more abstract concerns, such as the state of the nation. Even so, meaning can never be completely fixed, and readings of certain films as parables, say, or as moral tales, are undoubtedly available, especially where such readings are authorised by their conditions of production and reception.

Where Are My Children, for example, was constituted by the conditions under which it appeared in Britain as a 'film sermon' on the question of race suicide, never emerging as the riveting family melodrama it had been in the USA. At a meta-narrative level, *Fit to Fight* identifies freedom from disease with patriotism, suggesting that both are necessary prerequisites of a nation's victory in war. And in VD propaganda films in general, characters are invariably constructed as types in terms of their moral positions, or the positions they occupy as enunciators or recipients of narratively crucial knowledge. In these respects many of the films dealt with in this inquiry combine the concerns with the familial and the personal characteristic of popular fiction cinema of the day with a preoccupation with contemporary social and socio-sexual questions.

Cinema's active involvement in processes of discursivity is well illustrated by the ways in which fears about corruption in the socio-sexual sphere are articulated in these films. During the 1910s, anxieties about the corruption of the moral and physical integrity of the race/nation grounded both fears about a declining birth rate and also a moral panic about venereal disease. In the films, these concerns are seized upon, but are transformed – often beyond recognition – when they come into contact with the specific qualities of cinema as representation: with its conventions of narrativity and characterisation, and its properties as spectacle. In particular, in the production of meanings centring upon purity, specifically that female sexual purity with which fiction films of the period seem to be fascinated, not to say obsessed, cinema constructs corruption in opposition not so much to health or integrity as to a certain kind of innocence.

Alongside sexual innocence, however, *knowledge* can be posed as a counterforce to corruption. As I have noted, lack of certain kinds of knowledge typically structures the narratives of the films dealt with here – though the eventual provision of the absent knowledge can serve a variety of narrational ends. In a VD propaganda feature such as *Damaged Goods*, the downfall of the hero as a syphilis victim comes about as a direct result of his ignorance about venereal diseases and how they can be cured: a satisfactory resolution of the narrative demands that George Dupont obtain both knowledge and cure. Knowledge, therefore, is itself constituted as prophylactic. In another VD film, *The End of the Road*, this is even more explicit: sex education is urged as a means of preventing women from falling into 'disease and disgrace' as a result of ignorance. On the other hand, in *Maisie's Marriage*, a film informed more by sexology than by eugenics, knowledge of another sort – about birth control – is proposed as a prerequisite of a rather different narrative goal – personal and conjugal happiness.

But as long as a certain sexual innocence is also set up in these films as an object of desire, the construction of knowledge on sexual matters as narratively crucial opens up a space of contradiction between different discourses on corruption and its remedy. It is significant, as I shall explain below, that the question of female sexuality is centrally involved here, especially given that the period is marked by conflicts about the morality, desirability and utility of propagating information on sexual matters. These conflicts, waged against a background of struggle between the rival claims of various scientific and religious knowledges to the socio-sexual as an arena of inquiry and reform, are centred upon the problem of knowing about the body and its sexuality. Conducted on the terrain of cinema, they call forth relations of power which constitute cinema as a particular domain of regulation, so setting in play certain machineries of regulation.

Knowledge, power, cinema

The period under consideration in this inquiry is characterised by a series of rivalries, struggles even, between various forms of knowledge competing for pre-eminence in the discursive production of the sphere of the socio-sexual as a distinct object of inquiry and regulation. If the principal antagonists here were science and religion, there was also competition within each area. In the field of secular knowledge, in particular, eugenics and sexology both laid claim to scientificity, while each defined the socio-sexual in its own terms. But while the socio-sexual was constructed differently in various forms of knowledge, there was also a certain degree of accommodation between these knowledges. So, for instance, the objectives of social hygiene and social purity might be united in the activities of organisations devoted to social reform – the National Council of Public Morals being a case in point. Likewise, as is evident in their common advocacy of birth control, eugenists and sexologists increasingly came to share similar goals.

Rivalries nevertheless persisted: in particular, distinctions were frequently made between acceptable as against unacceptable knowledge about the body and its sexuality, and contending claims made, if not for the truth, certainly for the practical usefulness of different forms of knowledge.[13] If such struggles signal some broad interrelation of knowledge and power, an analysis of particular instances demonstrates more specifically how knowledge is produced within particular apparatuses and practices, and how these in turn are caught up in various strategies of power. Conflicts as to the truth and/or utility of specific knowledges, then, are institutionally implicated.

Was the source of 'proper' knowledge about the body and its sexuality to be the church, the medical profession, the Eugenics Society, the social purity movement, or the sex reform movement? Among the various discourses which staked their claims to the territory of the socio-sexual during the early part of this century, conflict prevailed not only over the contents and sources of 'proper' knowledge in the field, but also over the dissemination of such knowledge: where was it to be directed, and what was the most appropriate means of circulating it? If knowledge of the socio-sexual is institutionally implicated, so too is its social availability. Relations of power surrounding knowledge of the socio-sexual comprise both incitements and resistances, then, not only to the production, but also to the circulation, of such knowledge.

Cinema is caught up, at a number of levels and in a variety of often contradictory ways, in these power relations. For example, certain sources of knowledge of the socio-sexual are privileged over others in films. VD propaganda features in particular repeatedly stress the disastrous consequences for characters seeking a cure for their condition of relying on 'improper' forms of scientific or quasi-scientific knowledge. Only characters who consult qualified medical practitioners can be sure of a cure, while for those who go to 'quacks' – practitioners whose claims to scientific proficiency are constituted as spurious[14] – ruin of one kind or another is inevitable. In a different thematic context, the perversion of medical expertise is also condemned in the character of the abortionist Malfit in *Where Are My Children*. In *Maisie's Marriage*, on the other hand, the knowledge necessary to satisfactory narrative closure is provided not by a doctor but by a happily married, and presumably sexually satisfied, middle-class wife and mother, whose enunciative authority is guaranteed by life experience rather than by any specialised scientific knowledge.

If, at least at a surface level, the films dealt with in this inquiry are readable as speaking on behalf of particular sources of knowledge about the socio-sexual, such superficial readings are not necessarily exhaustive. In all of the films, socio-sexual knowledge of one sort or another is pertinent, even pivotal, to the progress of the narrative; and yet the narrative cannot propose any simple, fixed opposition between knowledge as desirable and its lack as undesirable, because the imperatives of cinematic representation get in the way. The narrative trajectory of knowledge is particularly prone to interruption on the part of female sexuality, or rather of constructs of female sexuality in the fiction cinema of the period – a cinema in which female sexual innocence and virginity are commonly reduced to one another and eroticised as 'purity'.

In their preoccupation with a sexual purity at constant risk, and with the moment of a sexually uninitiated young woman's fall from innocence, the films examined here are by no means untypical. The character of the housekeeper's daughter in *Where Are My Children* – whose seduction and fall lead ultimately to her death – exemplifies this tendency at its most extreme. However, if purity is commonly represented as contingent upon sexual ignorance, its construction as desirable must impede a narrative's impulse to knowledge. Any film which proposes not only sexual knowledge but also (where innocence equals ignorance) sexual innocence as desirable is obviously enmeshed in a contradiction. In many of the films considered here, both processes are indeed simultaneously at work: as propaganda, they privilege knowledge, while as popular fiction they sanction innocence/ ignorance. It is this hybrid quality, perhaps, which places most of these films at the margin of contemporary mainstream cinema.

The question of the nature of popular cinema links with that of the social availability of knowledge of the socio-sexual: the somewhat uneasy position of such knowledge *vis-à-vis* certain conventions of fiction cinema renders the latter rather problematic as a vehicle for the dissemination of the former. In fact, within the social purity and sex reform movements, there was a good deal of debate on this very issue. While in some quarters, cinema was regarded as a potentially useful means of reaching large numbers of people, in others it was seen as partly responsible for that very decline in moral standards against which purity campaigns were being mounted. So, for example, although VD films were sometimes promoted by organisations devoted to the elimination of sexually transmitted diseases, there was at the same time a good deal of resistance to this tactic within the sex reform and social purity movements themselves. To this extent, VD propaganda films cannot be regarded unproblematically as participating in an 'education for chastity' movement.[15]

A reluctance to countenance cinema as a means of disseminating socio-sexual knowledge could be justified by reference to certain 'problems' arising from the prevailing conditions of exhibition and reception of feature films. Since meaning is never finally fixed, a film may be open to a variety of readings – and in the case of films of the sort dealt with here, not all of them necessarily in accord with the intentions of those working for the cause of sex reform or moral enlightenment. Indeed, it was the possibility of unintended readings – especially readings of films for their pornographic, rather than for their educative or moral, value – which led most social purity and social hygiene campaigners to an increasingly cautious attitude towards cinema as an instrument for propagating their ideas. Commercial exhibition was considered particularly troublesome, precisely because in such circumstances readings of films could not easily be channelled in the desired direction. With private screenings, on the other hand, publicity remained under the control of sponsors rather than cinema proprietors, and audiences could be pre-selected and directed towards 'appropriate' readings by means of printed leaflets, talks and other supporting material. At the same time, though, such strategies for circumscribing meaning also effectively eliminated the main point in favour of commercial cinema: the large audiences it could command.

The films discussed in this study came to be constituted as troublesome in the degree to which they escaped certain attempts to direct their reading. Foremost among the problems presented by these films, when set loose in the relative semiotic free-for-all of the picture palace, was the sort of people who would be likely to see them – the cinema audience. During the period covered by this inquiry, the audience for commercial cinema was assumed to be comprised mainly of working-class people, among them large numbers of children and adolescents. Much of the concern expressed about the appropriateness of cinema as an instrument of moral and sexual reform turns precisely on the social composition of the audience for films. Were the working classes fit to receive knowledge of this kind? And if so, was the cinema the best way of disseminating it? What, after all, was commercial cinema *for*: entertainment or enlightenment?

Behind such questions lie two key assumptions of the period about the cinema and its audience. First, it was felt that certain groups in society – namely, the working classes, and working-class children especially – might easily be corrupted rather than enlightened by socio-sexual knowledge, especially when this was disseminated in the already morally questionable conditions of the public cinema. It was also assumed that knowledge in these areas, far from 'moralising' the infinitely corruptible lower classes, might actually incite them to immoral acts – might, in short, 'demoralise' them.

At a certain period, then, matters pertaining to the body and its sexuality were raised in fiction films, especially in films intended for commercial exhibition. To this extent, cinema took part in producing and circulating certain forms of knowledge of the socio-sexual, and consequently in that proliferation of discourses on sexuality which is said to mark this period. At the same time, however, such incitements produced resistances, ranging in this instance from a rejection of cinema as a vehicle for transmitting certain types of knowledge, to acts of censorship directed at particular films. This dual movement of incitement and resistance is condensed in the moment around the mid-1910s when the social purity movement became a site of struggle over understandings of cinema and its place in society: was cinema to be considered a threat to public morals, or a means of spreading moral enlightenment? Crucial in the resolution of this question was the discursive construction, at a specific juncture, of the cinema audience, and the processes through which cinema came to be constituted as a public sphere of regulation.

7 A New Public Sphere

From the censoring of films to the censoring of audiences is but a short step.

The Bioscope, 1917

Public and private

Having made its debut in the 1890s, cinema entered a certain public sphere of regulation in 1909 with the passage of the first Cinematograph Act. However, this legislation, far from settling the issue of cinema's place in the public sphere, effectively inaugurated a series of struggles over precisely that question. For at least a decade and a half, the question of how cinema was to be defined, understood, and in the final instance regulated, stood at the centre of an array of discourses, practices and powers which participated in a common – but contested – project of constituting this new medium. A good deal of uncertainty about what cinema was to become, and what was to become of cinema, marks the years between 1909 and 1925. Many of the struggles, the rivalries, the alliances – in short the power relations – at work in this period, as cinema was in process of constitution as a public sphere of regulation, reveal themselves in the case histories at the centre of this inquiry.

But if cinema was, for a time at least, 'up for grabs', it was eventually to take its place in the public sphere as a highly circumscribed object. Before considering how this came about, it might be useful to look briefly at some of the conditions under which specific formations of the public sphere are produced in particular instances. Such formations commonly claim to be grounded in the first place in a distinction between public and private. The public/private distinction effects a demarcation of areas of social life and social space, constructing them as mutually exclusive, self-evidently distinct from one another. It is commonly deployed in the service of ordering and classifying diverse forms of social organisation, appealing to an underlying or prior dualism. This, however, is not what is being proposed here.

For when the public/private opposition is traced in its specificity in concrete social-historical instances, it soon becomes clear that not only the content of each category, but also the site of the boundary between the categories, are potential sites of struggle. Even if at some abstract level the public and the private might be seen as constituting distinct domains, there will still be variations in actual social-historical instances as to what is held to belong in either category, and where the one is seen to stop and the other to begin. Public and private, in other words, are discursive constructs, produced differently in every one of the instances in which they operate as categories in opposition, and yet at the same time appealing to a universal distinction. These categories are to be understood, therefore, as *effects* of negotiation and contestation between discourses and powers in play in particular social, historical or cultural instances.

If there is any general ground for distinction between public and private spheres, it might be that the public constitutes the domain of legitimate social regulation while the private falls outside, or inhabits the fringes of, that domain. Although this may seem tautologus – whatever is public is in the field of regulation and whatever is in the field of regulation is public – such circularity can be dispensed with by considering specific constructs of public and private. For example, even within one system of thought – political philosophy – at least three understandings of the private sphere can be identified: a geographical notion of private space, an alignment of privacy with the person or her/his individuality, and an association between privacy and property or ownership.

The desire of each of these constructs of the private would be to place its contents outside the ambit of social regulation. And yet as constructs they can never be finally fixed: each is always negotiated, always in process. The boundaries between the public and the private, the regulated and the unregulated, then, are constantly shifting, constantly susceptible to challenge and reformulation. Thus, for instance, a liberal political philosophy might seek to determine the limits of the public sphere by appealing to certain notions of harm, arguing that only transitive harm – harm done by persons to others, say – justifies legal regulation. A conservative view, on the other hand, might hold that this particular harm condition is inadequate, because it excludes moral and social harm. Morality, according to such a view, is not a matter of individual choice, but rather a public issue, and so subject to regulation on grounds that a breach of the moral code constitutes an offence against the community.[1] Not only are different limits to the public sphere produced in different discourses, but these distinctions also call into play operations of power through which boundaries between public and private – and therefore strategies of regulation of the public – are negotiated. At stake, therefore, in the public/private distinction, and in the definitional struggles across the various discourses which construct it, is nothing less than the regulation of the social order.

During the period early in the present century when cinema was becoming established as a major leisure industry, it was also in process of becoming a public sphere, subject to regulation. The emergence of a public sphere of cinema was, however, contested: its creation involved struggles over both its character and its boundaries, struggles between different powers and various understandings of what cinema – both as industry and as representation – ought to be. Through these contestations cinema was *produced* as a particular public sphere of regulation. What, then, were the powers involved? How did they operate, and with what effects? In what ways was the public space that would be inhabited by cinema conceptualised during this formative period?

Initially, perhaps, cinema was regarded as a public sphere in the degree that films were consumed in public, as opposed to private, *places*: after 1909, films were increasingly exhibited in purpose-built picture palaces to which the general public could gain admittance simply on purchase of a ticket. In this context, cinema could be defined as a public sphere on the grounds that cinema buildings were places of public resort. Such an effectively spatial understanding of cinema's public sphere was enshrined in the earliest legislation relating to the medium, the Cinematograph Act of 1909. But the public/private opposition soon began to acquire additional inflections *vis-à-vis* cinema. In particular, a distinction on grounds of person informs certain debates about the users of cinema. This becomes most evident where the effects of cinema-going on the morals and conduct of cinema audiences is at issue.

In relation to cinema, then, the public/private opposition is constructed first of all in terms of the places in which films were consumed. Also important, however, is the constitution of consumers of films as inhabitants of a public sphere of regulation. Between cinema buildings on the one hand and the cinema-going public on the other lie actual films, representations seen as inhabiting a public sphere by virtue not only of the place, but also the manner, of their consumption. At a certain moment, all these would-be constituents of cinema's public sphere – buildings, persons, representations – became the target of a series of sometimes contradictory strategies directed at the definition and regulation of cinema. Various contending forces were at work in determining the nature of cinema's public sphere – what cinema was, what it was for, and how it was to be regulated. However, this process of definition, like any other, is exclusive as much as it is inclusive: if it aimed to settle the question of what cinema was, it would also determine what cinema was not. Power relations involved in the creation of the public sphere of cinema placed certain films, modes of consumption and relations of spectatorship outside the limits of that sphere, with the result that a circumscribed public sphere of cinema eventually became coterminous with cinema *tout court*.

A contested public sphere

The places in which films were shown were public in the sense that they were open to any passer-by choosing to walk in and buy a ticket. But if cinema-going involved economic exchange, film was a curious sort of commodity: the consumer purchased not the film itself as a physical object, but simply the right to sit for a while in a darkened auditorium watching shadows on a screen. Cinema's success as a business, however, depended exactly on this mode of consumption: one film was capable of simultaneous viewing by a large number of people, while for each projection of a single print of a film hundreds of tickets could be sold. If the pleasure obtained from viewing a film was an individual or a private matter, the conditions of its viewing made the act of spectatorship a public, if not necessarily a social, activity. And while the peculiar commodity status of films did not necessarily dictate that they be consumed in places of public resort, the imperatives of an industry founded upon a certain technology and devoted to the maximisation of profit certainly rendered the public commercial cinema a highly appropriate site for the consumption of its products and for the formation of its consumers.

While apparatuses of exhibition and consumption of films might be historically contingent, strategies for regulating cinema effectively endorsed a particular set of exhibition practices, so privileging certain modes of reception. Among the most significant of these strategies is undoubtedly the legal discourse embodied in the 1909 Cinematograph Act, which provided for controls over cinema buildings. Buildings were defined in the Act in terms of cinematographic technology: they were places where 'pictures or other optical effects' were exhibited 'by means of a cinematograph [projector], or other apparatus, for the purposes of which inflammable films are used'. Because the nitrate film stock in general use at the time was considered dangerously inflammable, it was argued that cinemas presented a special risk of fire. Certain controls over the places where films were shown were consequently seen as justifiable in the interests of public safety.

But legal discourse in this area was more complex and contradictory than would be suggested by an apparent concern with the physical safety of cinema-goers. This is due partly to the Cinematograph Act's incorporation of pre-existing approaches to the legal control of places of public entertainment, and partly to the way in which the statute itself was drafted. In the first instance, as places of public entertainment catering for the common people, cinemas were regarded, legally speaking, as comparable with music halls: the Cinematograph Act's provisions for local authority licensing of cinema buildings adopted, in essence, arrangements of the sort that had been in operation for some years for these particular public places. Second, the Cinematograph Act neither defined nor did it specify how safety was to be ensured, though the statutory instruments issued under it did give some guidance in this area.

Statute law – the Cinematograph Act – and delegated legislation – its statutory instruments – together framed the conditions under which cinema buildings were to be subject to legal regulation, constructing in the process a predominantly spatial definition of the public sphere inhabited by cinema. The machinery laid down by statute for effecting legal regulation of this sphere was to be a cinema licensing system administered by local authorities. This system, however, was active in its own right in constructing cinema's public sphere in ways which overlapped, and even at points conflicted with, the operations of statute and delegated legislation. For example, local licensing authorities soon began to impose licensing conditions unrelated to the safety, however broadly defined, of cinema buildings, including provisions as to the character of films shown on licensed premises. If controls over film content were never actually written into law, the practice of censoring films acquired legal sanction indirectly, following on judgments in a series of court actions which challenged local authorities' powers under the Cinematograph Act. These judgments indicated that local authorities were within their legal rights in imposing licensing conditions not strictly related to the safety of cinema buildings, and it was taken for granted – an assumption never directly challenged in law – that local licensing authorities' powers included the right to censor films. The cinema licensing system thus became the sole legal foundation of film censorship in Britain (see chapter 2).

To a certain extent, though, legal discourse was instrumental in producing diverse constructions of cinema's public sphere. For example, the move on the part of local cinema licensing authorities to prohibit films 'likely to be injurious to morality'[2] draws into a public sphere of regulation the moral welfare of cinema-goers, constituting it precisely as *public* morality. To this extent, the licensing system became the instrument of a certain legal moralism. Inasmuch as the objects of cinema's legal regulation ranged from the structural features and equipment of picture palaces, to the character of films, to the morals of the cinema-going public, cinema's public sphere was constituted in legal discourse as a rather heterogeneous object.

At the same time, the cinema licensing system inhabited a border ground between legal and extra-legal regulation. If the Cinematograph Act unquestionably enjoyed the authoritative status of legal discourse, while on the other hand the rules and procedures of the British Board of Film Censors, say, did not, between these two extremes lay a series of what might be termed 'quasi-legal' discourses – discourses which, while at moments laying claim to the discursive authority of law, actually bear a rather uneasy relation to it. In particular, the Home Office administrative circulars which advised local authorities on their implementation of the cinema licensing system (see chapter 2) occupy a highly ambiguous position *vis-à-vis* the processes of making and executing laws. While statute law and delegated legislation are backed by the authority of Parliament, regulative discourses emanating from the administration are not.[3] In practice, however, matters are rarely so clearcut. Circulars

> are not intended to be legislative in character and are issued, not under statutory authority, but for guidance. They may, however, contain legislative material:

which suggests that a distinction between legislation and administration is difficult to maintain in practice.[4] In the case of the Home Office circulars on film censorship, 'guidance' came from a department of state and was both unpublished and confidential: maximum authority, then, was thus combined with minimum public accountability.

During the period under consideration here, questions concerning the censorship of films were handled by the administration exclusively through 'advisory' circulars, a situation which betokens a split between machineries of regulation and objects of regulation. While the highly visible discourses of law were directed at cinema as a space, a place of public resort, films and their contents were targeted by lower profile – if nonetheless authoritative – discourses of regulation. The most publicly visible practices directed at regulating film content, notably those of the British Board of Film Censors, enjoyed no status whatever in law, ambiguous or otherwise.

The cinema licensing system bridged legal and extra-legal strategies of regulation in that it combined elements of both. For example, although *in abstracto* the licensing system was backed by law, certain conditions attaching to actual licences became a focus of legal disagreement. Significantly, test cases brought under the Cinematograph Act suggest that trouble arose exactly at the point at which licensing shifted away from the regulation of cinema buildings and towards the regulation of films shown in them, and of the consumers of those films. At a certain moment, therefore, the cinema licensing system, embodying diverse constructs of a public sphere of cinema, became a site of struggle over definitions of that sphere. Was the public sphere of cinema to be seen in purely spatial terms? Or was it to embrace also the representations on public view and the morals of the public viewing them?

During this period, strategies of definition and regulation of cinema were guided by assumptions about *who* cinema was for. It was not merely the public accessibility of places in which films were shown that rendered cinema susceptible to certain strategies of regulation, but also the class and age composition of the people frequenting those places. A preoccupation with the cinema audience might well in fact subtend the shift of regulative activity, already noted, from buildings to films, and the struggles surrounding this shift arguably betoken uncertainty over whether cinema was in process of becoming a proletarian or a bourgeois public sphere. If pre-existing structures and relations of social class were implicated in this process,[5] so also were those apparatuses and power relations more directly involved in the contest over the public sphere of cinema. In Britain, cinema's public sphere emerged in a series of alliances and rivalries involving not only legal and quasi-legal strategies of regulation, but also practices of film censorship institutions, of the film trade, and of social purity and social reform bodies. At the very centre of these various forces stood the cinema audience, which entered the public sphere of cinema not merely as cinema's public, but as its besetting problem.

If the cinema audience presented a problem, this was in part because it was discursively constructed around a series of fears: specifically, fears about the peculiar vulnerability of certain social groups to corruption. While, as noted in the last chapter, anxieties about the demoralisation of the entire nation were a prominent preoccupation of the first two decades of this century, cinema audiences were considered to be in especially grave danger in this area. Such anxieties draw into the public domain the very bodies and souls of cinema-goers, who were typically characterised as a proletarian mass, exceptionally corruptible because, uneducated and unsophisticated, they were incapable of making moral choices. A comment by the Home Office on plans to make a film version of *Damaged Goods* –

> the Cinema differs greatly from the Theatre: the audience is less intelligent and educated, and includes far more children and young people[6]

– is unambiguous in its affirmation of such an attitude.

Fears evoked by the working class as cinema audience were not confined to the supposedly demoralising character of the films they saw, but extended to the very circumstances in which they were seen. The crowding together of large numbers of people in dimly-lit auditoria, for instance, was regarded as conducive to the spread of epidemics, and also – more significantly – as an inducement to 'improper' conduct. Characteristic of this view is a statement made by the Edinburgh Chief Constable, and reported by the Cinema Commission of Inquiry in 1917, to the effect that ' "the darkness, combined with the low standard of morality of the individual" led to indecency'. During the late 1910s, the Home Office received a number of reports about 'improper' behaviour in cinemas, and some years later W. Joynson Hicks, as Home Secretary, was to recall that

> Numerous complaints were made at one period that the bad lighting prevalent in cinemas led to undesirable conduct among the audience and to improper behaviour towards children.[7]

Such anxieties were particularly strongly expressed in relation to young audiences: during the 1910s, the danger of sexual assaults on children in or near cinemas was frequently discussed, as was the risk of eyestrain and other physical damage to children caused by film viewing. So, for example, the report of an inquiry undertaken in 1917 by the Bradford Medical Officer of Health concludes, characteristically, with the observation that

> cinemagoing can affect the vision and mind of children, giving rise to visual and mental fatigue prejudicial to normal development, which if these displays are too frequently indulged in, is certain to lead in the end to a greater or less degree of organic defect.[8]

A conflation of children's physical health with their moral welfare is a mark of many such expressions of disquiet. A *Times* leader of 1915 on the question of children and the cinema refers, for instance, to 'the moral and physical dangers to which young children may be exposed if they are allowed unrestricted admission to cinematograph shows', while the primary concern of the Cinema Commission of Inquiry was children's 'health, intelligence and morals'. These were seen as equivalently and concomitantly susceptible to the deleterious effects of cinema-going.[9]

If children on the one hand and the adult working classes on the other were held, as audiences for films, to present particular problems, then working-class children were considered doubly troublesome. Apart from being exposed to the risk of 'demoralisation' inherent in cinema, children and adolescents of the working class were seen as peculiarly vulnerable to a whole range of other harms associated with cinema-going. It was feared, for one thing, that they might be tempted to imitate criminal acts shown in films: indeed, plans made in 1916 to institute a state-operated scheme of film censorship were justified precisely on grounds that the 'recent increase in juvenile delinquency' was attributable to 'demoralising cinematograph films'.[10] The vision of hordes of working-class adolescents roaming the streets after a night at the cinema gave rise to a number of fears, then: fears partly for their safety, moral and physical, but also about their predilection for disorderly or criminal conduct.

A number of the test cases under the Cinematograph Act were in fact brought as a result of attempts to deal with these 'problems' through the cinema licensing system. At issue, for example, in *Theatre de Luxe (Halifax) Ltd* v. *Gledhill* (1915) was a local authority's imposition of the regulation that children unaccompanied by adults should not be admitted to cinemas after 9p.m. Although this particular condition was ruled *ultra vires*, subsequent efforts to regulate children's attendance at cinemas and to limit their exposure to certain types of film (*Mills* v. *London County Council* [1925], for instance) met with greater success, vociferous opposition from film exhibitors notwithstanding. General concerns about the cinema audience were intensified in expressions of anxiety about the exposure of working-class children and young people to films. These groups were not only considered particularly prone to moral corruption, but were at the same time looked on as an active threat to public order. Cinema-going was quite evidently regarded as capable of causing a whole range of social evils, then, and behind many expressions of anxiety on this count lies a preoccupation with the integrity of the social order.

Concerns of this kind are instrumental in producing their own objects of regulation; and in this context cinema, as a set of social and economic relations governing the reception of films, is constituted as a public sphere of regulation by virtue of the class and the age composition of its audience.[11] Films were 'for' the working classes in general, and 'for' working-class children in particular, and were to be consumed in the public space of the picture palace. The censorship activities described in the case histories can be understood in the light of such a construction of the nature and limits of the public sphere of cinema, a construction which produces cinema as a particular kind of object of regulation. But if the audience was a key component of this construct, it was also rather an unknown quantity. Indeed, it was perhaps the very fact that so little was known, and so much assumed, about the cinema audience that rendered it the object of such obsessive concern. Its regulation demanded precisely that it be known about, and a significant element in the discursive construction and regulation of the cinema audience was exactly a quest for knowledge about it. This quest was to harness itself to an emergent science of the social.

For a period of some four or five years during the mid-1910s, anxieties about the 'problem' of the cinema and its audience reached a peak. During this time, new power relations – in the shape of the social purity/social hygiene/social reform/social science nexus identified in chapter 6 – entered the contest over the public sphere of cinema. These forces sustained the production of 'scientific' accounts of the cinema and its audience, knowledge which not only promised an impartial demystification of its objects, but also proposed solutions to the problems they posed. As has been noted, the earliest project of this sort in Britain was the 1917 Cinema Commission of Inquiry, undertaken under the aegis of a social purity organisation, the National Council of Public Morals. The Commission proposed looking into

> the physical, social, educational and moral influences of the cinema, with special reference to young people.

Here, the methodology of social science is allied with an aspiration to social reform in the cause of producing knowledge about the cinema audience.[12] If knowing involves mastery, then this attempt to find out about the cinema audience is clearly an exercise of power.

The inclusion of 'physical, social, educational and moral influences' within the terms of reference of this inquiry bespeaks an assumption that the moral and the social occupy similar terrain to, inhabit the same public sphere of regulation as, the physical. Such a construction of morality and society as concomitant objects of investigation and regulation is quite characteristic of the period. Not only social purity organisations, but also most social reform groups of the time – even 'progressive' ones – shared the view that morality was a matter of public concern, and could and should be subject to social regulation. While such opinions were not always associated with arguments in favour of the enforcement of morals, legal moralism did inform the regulation of films and their contents wherever prohibitions as to the character of films shown in public cinemas were written into cinema licensing conditions. The Cinema Commission of Inquiry's Report endorsed practices of this sort, even going so far as to recommend that state censorship should replace the existing 'voluntary' arrangements. The public morality lobby was to remain active for some years to follow, pressing for greater intervention in film censorship on the part of government and the law. Although they did not succeed in this particular objective, the influence of public morality pressure groups on practices of film censorship was to become considerable, especially during the 1930s.[13]

In the period with which this inquiry is concerned, though, the efforts of social purity and social reform movements with regard to cinema were directed not so much at tightening controls on films through strengthening the machinery of censorship as at raising the morale of the cinema-going public by improving the quality of what was on offer in cinemas: the conclusions and recommendations of the Cinema Commission of Inquiry make this quite clear. If, however, this was an effort to embourgeoisify the new medium, it met with a certain amount of resistance. The precise nature of that resistance reveals itself in the case histories.

For example, efforts on the part of social purity and social reform movements to use fiction films and commercial cinema as a means of informing the public about 'social problems' such as venereal disease (chapter 4) encountered censorships which were instrumental not so much in determining the content of individual films as in setting boundaries to the public sphere of cinema. And the *Where Are My Children* affair (chapter 3) suggests that while efforts on the part of social purity movements to enhance the respectability of cinema were welcomed at first by a film trade eager to improve its discreditable public image, the recruitment of cinema to social and moral reform also constituted a potential threat to another of the industry's goals – profit. Consequently, opposition within the trade to the practice of exhibiting 'propaganda' films in commercial cinemas very soon began making itself felt.

Against the background of such rivalries, differences arose as to whether cinema should entertain its audience, or seek to 'improve' it. The view, embodied in discourses and practices of both the film trade and film censorship, that cinema's task was to entertain came up against the notion, embodied in discourses of social purity and social hygiene, that cinema could be harnessed to the 'good and high motives' of moral enlightenment and social reform. At the same time, however, while censorship and social purity might produce divergent understandings of cinema, they concurred in the view that cinema, however defined, was a problem demanding urgent attention; this in turn was strongly resisted by the film trade. Was cinema a problem, then, or was it not? And if it was a problem, what was to be done?

Cinema as domain of regulation

I have suggested that at a certain conjuncture, the 'problem' presented by cinema was laid at the door of its audience. How, then, was the cinema-going public, as a crucial constituent of an emergent public sphere, to be dealt with? Answers to this question are embedded in the diverse, if at points overlapping, understandings of cinema and its audience produced through the various relations of power in play in the contest over cinema's public sphere. As far, for example, as social purity and social reform were concerned, the audience was first of all to be known about – investigated, understood – and then it was to be improved. For the film trade, on the other hand, the audience – despite its regrettable lack of respectability – was to be left alone to enjoy, whenever it chose, whatever films it wished to see:

> Why hinder a great and growing industry whose business it is to give rest and relaxation to the toilers in munition factories, workshops and warehouses, to give entertainment and amusement to our soldiers, and to bring into the lives of hundreds of thousands of homes the only cheering prospect in the drab and colourless day, the thought of a visit to the cinema in the evening?[14]

If the cinema audience is ceaselessly spoken about during this period, it seldom speaks for itself. Its voice is filtered in the record through other discourses – those of governments, social purity, the film trade. Nevertheless, despite the virtual silence of the cinema audience on its own account, and despite the passive position it occupies as an object of discourse, its instrumentality in the events described here does emerge in some degree. The three case histories highlight the participation of legal, quasi-legal and extra-legal discourses and practices of film censorship in the construction of a particular public sphere of cinema during the formative period between 1909 and the mid-1920s. But they also bring to light the active involvement of the cinema audience in the constitution of cinema's public sphere as a commercialised leisure pursuit involving the consumption of fiction films for recreation, in places of public resort frequented by a proletarian mass incorporating large numbers of children and adolescents.

At the same time, though, the cinema audience constantly troubles this emergent public sphere, threatening instability, uncontrollability. If not already corrupted, it was seen as particularly susceptible to corruption. In either case, it would be highly volatile and prone to immoral, socially disruptive, even criminal, behaviour. In discourses and practices of film censorship, the cinema, its troublesome working-class audience, and 'entertainment' go hand-in-hand. This ensemble becomes the object of regulative strategies directed not only at the content of films but also at the conduct of cinema-goers.

But as long as the public sphere of cinema was contested, constructs of it embodied in discourses and practices of film censorship could hardly be determining: indeed, the very activities of censorship detailed in this book could only operate as outcomes of challenges to these constructs. These censorships are active, in other words, in the space of conflict between the various forces involved in producing definitions of cinema's public sphere. If censorship is *productive* in the sense that a certain public sphere of cinema is created through its discourses and practices, then so also is it a *product* in the sense that it is generated in the moment of resistance to the very definitions and regulative strategies it proposes.

8   Rethinking Film Censorship

What can you do but disrupt a history and re-create it as another history?

Juliet Mitchell, 1984

Prohibition and production

Historical and sociological studies of film censorship have invariably emphasised its institutional and prohibitive aspects, constructing it as an activity on the part of specific organisations – organisations whose avowed objective is to impose controls on films, usually by excluding from them themes, topics and images deemed for one reason or another unacceptable. Although it cannot be denied that film censorship can and does operate in this way, this inquiry indicates that a great deal more is at stake in the censorship of films than cuts, bans and boards of censors.

In each of the instances of censorship examined in the case histories, a complex set of practices and processes can be seen at work. By no means all of these emanate from organisations with a specific remit to censor, nor are they all necessarily prohibitive in their effects. These cases have some common ground in that similar sorts of operations are traceable across all three instances; but each one, with its unique configuration of processes and practices, is nevertheless quite distinct. My inquiry has aimed to attend to the complexity of these configurations, and, in combining certain investigative strategies with particular objects of inquiry, has sought to move beyond the prohibition/institutions models of film censorship. For while on one level this study can be read simply as amplifying the number and operational scope of institutions and prohibitions involved in the censorship of films, in the final instance it does something more than this: it challenges the very premises on which the prohibition/institutions model is grounded.

Such a challenge emerges most clearly in relation to institutions, in the conclusion that institutional practices of censorship are not confined to censoring organisations. By the same token, the activities of such organisations do not necessarily determine the nature and effectivity of specific acts of censorship. In Britain in the years between 1909 and 1925, a series of institutions – local cinema licensing authorities, the Home Office, the film trade, social purity and social reform movements, as well as the British Board of Film Censors itself – was implicated, in different ways and under different conditions, in processes of film censorship. But it is not merely a question of *which* institutions are caught up in any one instance of censorship: each instance is produced in its historical specificity in the *interactions* between the various institutional practices involved. To this extent, the object of inquiry becomes not simply the content – nor even the activities – of particular institutions, but the relations between them, the ensemble of practices condensed in any one instance of censorship.

Film censorship is a matter of relations, then: it is a process, not an object. Film censorship is not reducible to a circumscribed and predefined set of institutions and institutional activities, but is produced within an array of constantly shifting discourses, practices, and apparatuses. It cannot, therefore, be regarded as either fixed or monolithic. The struggles, rivalries and alliances which come to light in each of the instances analysed in this book suggest, on the contrary, that film censorship is an ongoing process embodying complex and often contradictory relations of power. Hence the specific instrumentality *vis-à-vis* film censorship of rival claims to epistemological pre-eminence on the part of different knowledges about the socio-sexual (chapter 6), and, more broadly, of conflicts over the nature of the emergent public sphere of cinema (chapter 7). These relations, furthermore, may be creative as much as repressive in their effects; and while practices directed at prohibition are prone to unanticipated consequences, much more than the merely unexpected may be at stake.

During the period under consideration here, film censorship participated, in conjunction with other apparatuses and practices, in the production of cinema as a public sphere of a particular kind. This constitutive process necessarily involved the drawing of boundaries around that sphere, and this in turn set limits to the terms under which cinema was dealt with in public discourse. Moves to keep 'health propaganda' films out of commercial cinemas can be understood in this light, as can the assumption underlying this prohibition that certain topics were not appropriate for a medium directed at a largely working-class and youthful audience. In this respect, film censorship obviously has a prohibitive logic. But at the same time, acts of prohibition produce their own objects. For example, the BBFC's policy of refusing to certificate propaganda films depended upon a construction of limits to cinema's public sphere, limits beyond which the newly-created genre was then placed. The propaganda film's outlaw status, then, is a production which licences a prohibition. In this context, therefore, prohibition and productivity may be regarded not as opposites, nor as mutually exclusive, but as two sides of the same coin.

Gestures of prohibition can produce unintended consequences: the wide-spread publicity received by the film *Maisie's Marriage*, to take just one example, was a direct consequence of efforts to suppress it. At the same time, prohibitions may also be effects of discursive productions. The constitution of cinema as a medium of entertainment for the working classes effectively sanctioned prohibitions on films which proved problematic in relation to this definition, perhaps by addressing the 'wrong' kind of audience in the 'wrong' way: propaganda films are a case in point here. Film censorship, then, incorporates production and prohibition in a relation of mutual dependence.

All of the apparatuses and instances of regulation examined in the present inquiry operate in a play of production and prohibition. The concept of regulation itself bespeaks such an interaction: for it is not an imposition of rules upon some pre-existing entity, but a process of constituting objects from and for its own practices. To speak in terms of regulation is also to signal a shift away from a prohibition/institutions model of film censorship towards a more intricate and kaleidoscopic approach. If it is accepted that film censorship comprises an ensemble of interrelated institutions, practices and discourses participating in complex and potentially contradictory relations of power, it becomes impossible – in the present instance, at least – to conceptualise power itself as monolithic, determining or wholly repressive. The notion of regulation captures not only the instrumental and processual character of the power relations involved in institutional practices surrounding film censorship, then, but also the simultaneously productive and prohibitive logic of their operation.

Strategies of regulation may be productive in other senses, too, for they are capable of generating resistances. If film censorship creates censorable films, then it can also call forth transgressions of the boundary between the acceptably representable and (to use the BBFC's term) the 'prohibitive' in film content. In this sense, censorship incites resistances, which in turn may provoke further gestures of censorship directed at maintaining the boundaries under challenge. Censorship, then, is an ongoing activity of definition and boundary-maintenance, produced and re-produced in challenges to, and transgressions of, the very limits it seeks to fix. The site of these limits and the degree of their fluidity are effects of the activity, at any particular moment, of the various relations of power and resistance involved.

Such an understanding of resistance and its productivity sheds a good deal of light upon the instances of censorship examined here. For example, implicit in the aspirations of social hygiene and social purity movements during the mid- to late 1910s to harness cinema to their objectives of racial regeneration and moral enlightenment is a move towards *embourgeoisement* of the new medium: not only might the existing audience for films be 'improved', but a new and more respectable one created as well. But, as indicated in chapters 3 and 6, this move encountered resistances of various kinds, despite initial support from a film trade anxious to acquire a less unprepossessing image for itself.

These resistances are to be understood in light of the fact that cinema's public sphere was being constructed largely in terms of class: cinema, that is, was seen as a medium 'for' a working-class audience. While this audience might have been regarded in some quarters as a 'problem', and while the film trade might have wished for a less disreputable public image than – largely due to its clientele – it suffered, the position occupied by a working-class audience in constructs of cinema's public sphere seems to have been unassailable. Attempts to raise the tone of the medium met with opposition precisely because they presented a challenge to notions about its class character.

However, while emergent definitions of cinema might seek to construct its consumers as largely working class, such an audience – itself a site of resistance to strategies of regulation – was to prove extremely troublesome. As such, it became all the more a target of regulation. If the cinema audience was a problem, this was partly because of the peculiar characteristics of film's mode of consumption. The fascinating qualities of the moving photographic image, especially as viewed from a comfortable seat in a darkened auditorium, have provoked comment since the earliest days of cinema. When an audience, as a social group, is caught up in the pleasure of watching a film, it becomes a gathering of spectators. The nub of the problem posed by cinema, perhaps, was this indefinable moment when an already troublesome social audience became subject to the power and fascination of the cinematic image – when, that is, audiences entered into a relationship, as spectators, with film texts.[1]

In many studies of censorship, film texts figure most prominently as objects of rules directed at 'drawing lines' – establishing and policing the limits of what, at any particular time, is representable. These rules may be embodied in lists of forbidden themes and subjects, such as those enumerated in 'O'Connor's 43', the informal censorship code which the BBFC began using in the late 1910s.[2] With such codes, rules of exclusion can be applied to individual films, and cuts requested where the rules would call for them. To the extent that they create censorable films, such exercises in boundary setting obviously have their own productivity. But looked at in another way, efforts of this sort are doomed to failure, if only because they construct their objects, film texts, as carriers of fixed meanings, when meaning is not actually inherent in films, but is produced in the process of their consumption.

If meaning in films emerges as much in their reception – in the relationship between films and their consumers, in other words – as in their content, film censorship is always faced with the difficulty that prohibitions directed at the contents of individual films could turn out to be off target. The 'problem' presented by cinema and its users is more than a problem of 'prohibitive' as against acceptable representations, therefore: it has to do also with the use of representations, with audiences and with modes of consumption. But while this might make cinema an elusive object of regulation, it also provokes – precisely as a response to such elusiveness – intensified efforts at regulation. This, perhaps, would explain why, throughout its history, cinema seems to have attracted more censorship than any pre-existing medium.[3]

Short of blanket prohibition, however, film censorship might seek to circumvent the difficulties posed by attempts to deal with the specificities of film content by directing its efforts towards readings of films. Readings are inevitably informed by the circumstances in which films are consumed, and by what the social audience brings to the activity of viewing by way of prior knowledge or 'cultural capital'. The BBFC's refusal to certificate propaganda films provides an instance of this kind of strategy. The outcome of such a prohibition, had it been entirely effective, would have been to limit the exhibition of propaganda features to non-commercial venues. These surroundings – in combination with the fact that the audience in such circumstances would probably have been a relatively 'respectable' one – would solicit readings of the films for their educational value, whilst reducing the likelihood of their being consumed as pornography.

That censorships of this sort might not, however, always produce the consequences intended is amply demonstrated by the case of *Maisie's Marriage*. The BBFC's demands that the film's original title, *Married Love*, be changed and its association with Marie Stopes downplayed in publicity material were clearly directed at limiting readings of the film: devoid of its link with Stopes and her 'notorious' book, *Maisie's Marriage* would be no more scandalous than any ordinary love story. In the event, though, it proved impossible to effect such a dissociation. This case signals not only the instrumentality of the cinema audience's cultural capital in the reception of films, but also indicates that in certain circumstances strategies of censorship directed at films and cinema are unable to cover all of the circumstances under which readings are generated.

At a certain conjuncture, film censorship was produced in the space of resistances to emergent definitions of the public sphere of cinema. The *Maisie's Marriage* affair suggests that censorship could also be incited by other resistances: notably by 'improper' readings of films. Censorship was provoked here not so much by transgression of the boundaries of cinema's public sphere, nor indeed of prohibitions on film content, as by a breach of certain extra-cinematic censorships (notably taboos on public discussion of sex and birth control). This transgression had its effects at the level not of the film text, but of its reading, for it was the cinema audience's cultural capital that licensed 'improper' readings of this film. The spectacularly unsuccessful efforts of the BBFC and the Home Office were aimed at inhibiting such readings by restricting the audience's access to certain types of knowledge.

The distinction which emerged around 1917, in the context of notions about cinema's 'social function', between entertainment and enlightenment also informed strategies directed at regulating readings of films. As noted in the cases of censorship discussed in chapters 3 and 4, it was this distinction which underlay attempts to prevent the public exhibition of propaganda films. However, resistances not so much to a distinction between entertainment and enlightenment as to the exclusion of the latter from the public sphere of cinema did ensure that at least some propaganda films received commercial exhibition. This challenge to the would-be limits of an emergent public sphere of cinema provoked moves to protect those limits: these took the form of renewed gestures of censorship.

The cycle of boundary construction-resistance-prohibition-resistance, as it emerges in these two cases, signals the active and processual character of film censorship. Film censorship ceases to be a series of isolated once-and-for-all acts of exclusion which always have whatever prohibitive effects might be intended and becomes instead a process of negotiation between contending powers, apparatuses and discourses. The long-running saga of VD propaganda films is a good case in point. This subcategory of the propaganda genre survived, from its beginnings in the middle and late 1910s, well into the 1930s: this could hardly have been possible had institutions of censorship been monolithic and practices of censorship decisive. In fact, over a period of some twenty years, a continuous play of resistance and regulation generated an entire set of institutional infrastructures for the circulation and exhibition of these supposedly 'prohibitive' films (chapter 4). In this instance at least, censorship actually became a necessary condition for the survival of a subgenre of censorable representations.

Film censorship and power

As well as exposing the interrelations of prohibition and productivity in particular instances of film censorship, the case histories also highlight the nature of the relations of power involved: these were exceptionally provisional during the period under consideration in this study. A shifting array of forces was involved in film censorship, and various resistances and countercensorship were produced in the rivalries and alliances between them. For example, for virtually the whole of the period – and particularly in the five or six years immediately following the passage of the 1909 Cinematograph Act – relations between the exhibition arm of the film trade on the one hand, and the local cinema licensing authorities on the other, were extremely uneasy. The principal bone of contention was the interpretation of the cinema licensing provisions in the new Act. The film trade – initially in favour of the Act – started objecting to local authorities' use of it to impose licensing conditions which bore no relation to safety in cinemas. A series of court cases between 1911 and 1925 centred on conflicts between the trade and licensing authorities over the legal powers of the latter.

A few years after its first resort to the courts, the film trade entered into open conflict with the government on the issue of state censorship, a proposal for which was put forward in 1916 by the Home Secretary. This scheme prompted objections from the trade, largely on grounds that it would constitute an unwarranted interference with business. On this same issue, the government was also at odds, though rather less publicly so, with the British Board of Film Censors: the new censorship scheme was necessary, the Home Office implied, because the BBFC was not doing its job properly. The film trade, as has been noted, eventually got its way on this question, and the BBFC was saved. Nevertheless, relations between the Board and the Home Office were to remain somewhat difficult for several years. It was not until the mid-1920s that the BBFC's position became relatively secure *vis-à-vis* both the government and local licensing authorities.

Just as the Board of Censors was recovering from the crisis over official censorship and was entering a period of trial under the leadership of its new president, T. P. O'Connor, it came into conflict with the social purity and social hygiene movements over propaganda films. The reformers wanted to educate the film-going public on questions of morality and sexuality, but the BBFC regarded such a move as a potential threat to its already precarious position. Films dealing with such issues were bound to be controversial, and the last thing the Board wanted was attention of that sort. It consequently adopted a policy of refusing to certificate propaganda films. Although it may appear strange that film censors would oppose efforts to 'improve' cinema and its audience, this particular clash is perfectly understandable in the light of the BBFC's overriding objective of self-preservation. There were undoubtedly other considerations at work here, too, in particular the Board's complicity in a definition of cinema as a medium dedicated to the diversion and amusement of the working classes. The exhibition of propaganda films in commercial cinemas, however worthy their sponsors and objectives, constituted a challenge to such a construct.

Also on the face of it somewhat unlikely is the alliance, short-lived as it was, between moral and social reformers and the film industry on exactly this issue of 'improving' the cinema audience. When social purity organisations began sponsoring propaganda films in the mid-1910s, the trade backed their efforts. This support, however, gave way to an acceptance of the BBFC's line as soon as it became clear that respectability could prove costly for business. Alliances as well as conflicts, then, were the order of the day. These relations were in a constant state of flux: in particular, over the entire period between 1909 and 1925, relations between the BBFC, the Home Office and the local licensing authorities were never stable.

These kaleidoscopically shifting allegiances and rivalries produced openings for resistance to various strategies of regulation of cinema, censorship included. Resistances emerge in the space of contradictions between the various forces involved in the production and regulation of a public sphere of cinema. The events described in the three case histories at the centre of this inquiry are certainly characterised by a fluidity of relations of power and resistance. In these instances at least, it is clear that the operations of the various institutions and institutional practices involved in the censorship of films were complex and overdetermined, and that acts of censorship might be productive as well as, even perhaps more than, prohibitive in their effects.

While an approach of this sort might usefully be deployed in investigations of film censorship in social-historical circumstances other than those considered here, it is nonetheless important to bear in mind the historical specificity of this inquiry, for it deals with a particularly formative period both for cinema and for film censorship, a period in which relations between contending forces were more fluid than they would ever be in later years. In a sense, the entire period constitutes a moment of risk, for cinema was still in many respects 'up for grabs'. Indeed, one of the main reasons for ending the investigation in the mid-1920s is that this was an important moment of accommodation between key contending forces. When the Home Office circulated its new recommended licensing conditions in 1923, and when the final judgment in *Mills* v. *London County Council* was given in 1925, the Home Office, the local licensing authorities and the British Board of Film Censors moved together towards mutual accord. While this did not necessarily herald an end to all conflict, it did introduce some degree of hegemony into a previously fragmented set of power relations.

At the same time, the social purity movement, having largely abandoned the strategy of using commercial cinema to propagate its ideas, maintained active involvement in questions of cinema and censorship well into the 1930s. Although some sections of the movement came to exert some influence on policies and practices of film censorship, others met with a certain amount of opposition.[4] It is unlikely, moreover, that the film trade stopped advancing its own cause as soon as the BBFC, in alliance with local licensing authorities and the Home Office, secured a decisive enhancement of its own authority – though it might well have become more difficult at this point for the trade to influence events. Notwithstanding, the fact remains that at a certain conjuncture key forces involved in struggles over the definition and regulation of cinema entered into an authoritative alliance. At this moment the power relations of film censorship in Britain entered a new phase. If still by no means monolithic, these powers became less provisional and more hegemonic than ever before. The moment of risk was over.

If any general conclusion about film censorship and power can be drawn from this inquiry, it must be that it is unwise to suppose that the forces involved in film censorship at any conjuncture are in any way fixed or decisive. Such an assumption, since it does not so much raise questions as suggest answers in advance, would in any case make historical inquiry redundant. This is not to deny that in certain social-historical circumstances film censorship might operate hegemonically. The question for the historian, however, must be: under precisely what conditions has it done so, or might it do so? In other words, establishing degrees of hegemony and homogeneity on the one hand, or of fluidity and provisionality on the other, must be the objective, not the starting point, of inquiry. Such an approach permits examination and analysis of the forces involved in film censorship in different historical circumstances, of the interactions of these forces, and thus of the nature of, and potential for, changes in these relations of power.

Notes and References

1 Investigating Film Censorship

1 Dorothy Knowles, *The Censor, the Drama and the Film, 1900–1934* (London: Allen & Unwin, 1934), pp. 169–74. See also Ivor Montagu, *The Political Censorship of Films* (London: Gollancz, 1939): during the 1930s, the BBFC refused to certificate Soviet films, including *Battleship Potemkin* and *Mother*. John Trevelyan, *What the Censor Saw* (London: Michael Joseph, 1973), chapters 1 and 2. See also Guy Phelps, *Film Censorship* (London: Gollancz, 1975), chapter 2. The Festival of Light's viewpoint on censorship is put forward in Longford Committee, *Pornography: The Longford Report* (London: Coronet Books, 1972): in the mid-1970s, publicly exhibited films were, for the first time ever, subjected to legal action on grounds of indecency. United Kingdom, Home Office, *Report of the Committee on Obscenity and Film Censorship*, Cd. 7772 (London: HMSO, 1979). Debates on censorship have been reactivated in the 1980s, though with less concern about cinema than about television and home video.

2 For the 1909–25 period, see Rachael Low, *The History of the British Film, 1906–1914* (London: Allen & Unwin, 1949), pp. 84–90; Rachael Low, *The History of the British Film, 1914–1918* (London: Allen & Unwin, 1950), pp. 126–41; Rachael Low, *The History of the British Film, 1918–1929* (London: Allen & Unwin, 1971), pp. 55–70; Ernest Betts, *The Film Business: A History of British Cinema, 1896–1972* (London: Allen & Unwin, 1973), pp. 47–50.

3 Neville March Hunnings, *Film Censors and the Law* (London: Allen & Unwin, 1967). Other considerations of film censorship from a legal standpoint include Neville Hunnings, 'Cinematograph and indecent displays', *Sight and Sound* 43 (Winter 1973–4), pp. 26–7; Neville Hunnings, 'Restrictions – more or less?' *Sight and Sound* 46 (Autumn 1977), p. 217; Geoffrey Robertson, 'The future of film censorship', *British Journal of Law and Society* 7 (1980), pp. 78–94. On the US, see Ira H. Carmen, *Movies, Censorship and the Law* (Ann Arbor: University of Michigan Press, 1966).

4 Nicholas Pronay, 'The first reality: film censorship in liberal England', in *Feature Films as History*, edited by K. R. M. Short (London: Croom Helm, 1981), pp. 113–37; Jeffrey Richards, 'The British Board of Film Censors and content control in the 1930s: images of Britain', *Historical Journal of Film, Radio and Television* 1 (1981), pp. 95–116; Jeffrey Richards, 'The BBFC and content control in the 1930s: foreign affairs', *Historical Journal of Film, Radio and Television* 2 (1982), pp. 39–48; Nicholas Pronay, 'The political censorship of films in Britain between the wars', in *Propaganda, Politics and Film, 1918–48*, edited by Nicholas Pronay and D. W. Spring (London: Macmillan, 1982), pp. 98–125: James C. Robertson, 'British film censorship goes to war', *Historical Journal of Film, Radio and Television* 2 (1982), pp. 49–64; Nicholas Pronay and Jeremy Croft, 'British film censorship and propaganda policy during the Second World War', in *British*

Cinema History, edited by James Curran and Vincent Porter (London: Weidenfeld & Nicolson, 1983), pp. 144–63; Jeffrey Richards, *The Age of the Dream Palace: Cinema and Society in Britain, 1930–1939* (London: Routledge & Kegan Paul, 1984), part 2; James C. Robertson, *The British Board of Film Censors: Film Censorship in Britain, 1896–1950* (London: Croom Helm, 1985). The fact that in Britain (unlike, say, the United States) the majority of, and perhaps the most important, historical work on film censorship has been done by political historians rather than by historians of cinema says a great deal about the formation and academic institutionalisation of knowledge in each country.

5 On the former, see Edward de Grazia and Roger K. Newman, *Banned Films: Movies, Censors and the First Amendment* (New York: R. R. Bowker, 1982), on film censorship in the USA; and on British censorship, more impressionistically, see Trevelyan, *What the Censor Saw*. On the latter see, for example, James C. Robertson, 'Dawn (1928): Edith Cavell and Anglo-German relations', *Historical Journal of Film, Radio and Television* 4 (1984), pp. 15–28.

6 This tendency, as it affects certain approaches in cultural studies, is discussed by Raymond Williams, in 'Base and superstructure in Marxist cultural theory', *New Left Review* 82 (1973), pp. 3–16. For a debate about its implications for work in the history of cinema, see Andrew Higson, 'Critical theory and "British cinema"', *Screen* 24, 4–5 (1983), pp. 80–95; reply by Vincent Porter, *Screen* 25, 1 (1984), pp. 86–7; rejoinder by Andrew Higson, *Screen* 25, 1 (1984), p. 88.

7 See, for example, Geoffrey H. Hartman, ed., *Psychoanalysis and the Question of the Text* (Baltimore: Johns Hopkins University Press, 1978); Josue V. Harari, *Textual Strategies: Perspectives in Post-Structuralist Criticism* (London: Methuen, 1980); Robert Young, ed., *Untying the Text* (London: Routledge & Kegan Paul, 1981); Robert Scholes, *Semiotics and Interpretation* (New Haven: Yale University Press, 1982). Attempts within these perspectives to conceptualise textual operations in a social/historical frame (for example by attempting to incorporate analyses of reception, or by treating texts as social discourses) tend to fall back into a privileging of the textual: for example, see Edward Said, *Orientalism* (London: Routledge & Kegan Paul, 1978); Susan R. Suleiman and Inge Crosman, eds, *The Reader in the Text: Essays on Audience and Interpretation* (Princeton: Princeton University Press, 1980).

8 See David Bordwell, 'Textual analysis, etc.', *Enclitic*, 5/6 (1981–2), pp. 125–36. In David Bordwell, Janet Staiger and Kristin Thompson, *The Classical Hollywood Cinema: Film Style and Mode of Production to 1960* (London: Routledge & Kegan Paul, 1985), 'style' and 'mode of production' are dealt with in separate chapters. Robert C. Allen and Douglas Gomery, in *Film History: Theory and Practice* (New York: Alfred A. Knopf, 1985), distinguish between aesthetic film history, technological film history, economic film history, and social film history.

9 Michel Foucault, 'The confession of the flesh', in *Power/Knowledge* (Brighton: Harvester Press, 1980), pp. 194–228 (p. 194; p. 196).

10 Michel Foucault, *Discipline and Punish: The Birth of the Prison* (Harmondsworth: Penguin, 1977), p. 26.

11 Michel Foucault, *The History of Sexuality, Volume 1: An Introduction* (New York: Pantheon Books, 1978), p. 82; Hubert L. Dreyfus and Paul Rabinow, *Michel Foucault: Beyond Structuralism and Hermeneutics* (Chicago: University of Chicago Press, 1982), chapter 5. See also Michel Foucault, 'The subject and power', *Critical Inquiry* 8 (1982), pp. 777–95 (p. 793).

12 Foucault, 'The confession of the flesh', p. 196; *Discipline and Punish*, p. 27.

13 See, for example, Michel Foucault, 'Truth and Power', in *Power/Knowledge*, pp. 109–33.

14 Allen and Gomery, *Film History*, pp. 16–20; Roy Bhaskar, *A Realist Theory of Science* (Atlantic Highlands, N.J.: Humanities Press, 1978).

15 Michel Foucault, 'Questions of Method', *Ideology and Consciousness*, 8 (1981), pp. 3–14 (p. 6); Foucault, *Discipline and Punish*. See also Michel Foucault, 'Nietzsche, genealogy, history' in *Language, Counter-Memory, Practice* (Oxford: Basil Blackwell, 1977), pp. 139–64. If there is a distinction to be drawn between Bhaskar's Realist approach on the one hand, and Foucault's *post hoc* explanation of his own historiographic procedures on the other, this perhaps lies in the former's posing of description and analysis as separate procedures. However, the similarity of the two approaches consists most especially in their common argument that the object of historical inquiry ought properly to be events (or as Goucault calls them elsewhere, 'cultural instances').

2 The Birth of Film Censorship in Britain

1 Michel Foucault, *The History of Sexuality, Volume 1: An Introduction* (New York: Pantheon Books, 1978), pp. 92–3.

2 On early practices of film exhibition in Britain, see Rachael Low and Roger Manvell, *The History of the British Film, 1896–1906* (London: Allen & Unwin, 1948), chapter 4; Rachael Low, *The History of the British Film, 1906–1914* (London: Allen & Unwin, 1949), chapter 1. Statistics on cinema audiences for this period are rare, and possibly unreliable. Those cited here are taken from Philip Corrigan, 'Film entertainment as ideology and pleasure; a preliminary approach to a history of audiences', in *British Cinema History*, edited by James Curran and Vincent Porter (London: Weidenfeld & Nicolson, 1983), pp. 24–35. On the American penetration of the British market, see Michael Chanan, 'The emergence of an industry', in Curran and Porter (eds), *British Cinema History*, pp. 39–58; Kristin Thompson, *Exporting Entertainment: America in the World Film Market, 1907–34* (London: British Film Institute, 1985), Table A.II, p. 215. On the Cinematograph Films Act, see Margaret Dickinson and Sarah Street, *Cinema and State: the Film Industry and the British Government, 1927–84* (London: British Film Institute, 1985), chapter 1.

3 Neville March Hunnings, *Film Censors and the Law* (London: Allen & Unwin, 1967), p. 35: a detailed account of the pre-1909 legal situation with regard to cinema may be found on pp. 29–39.

4 Hunnings, *Film Censors and the Law*, pp. 39–43.

5 Hunnings, *Film Censors and the Law*, p. 45. See also James C. Robertson, *The British Board of Film Censors: Film Censorship in Britain, 1896–1950* (London: Croom Helm, 1985), p. 2.

6 House of Commons debates, vol. 3, cols. 1596–7 (21 April 1909).

7 Cinematograph Bill considered in committee, House of Commons debates, vol. 9, cols. 2260–66 (25 August 1909); report stage, House of Commons debates, vol. 10, cols. 329–37 (31 August 1909); House of Lords debates, vol. 3, cols. 17–18 (20 September 1909). On the seriousness or otherwise of the fire hazard, see Hunnings, *Film Censors and the Law*, p. 44. Robertson suggests that Samuel 'greatly exaggerated the danger of cinema fires to evade too probing a Commons discussion': *The British Board of Film Censors*, p. 3. Within the Act's first eighteen months, the Home Office was notified of two cinema fires – both caused by electrical faults rather than by inflammable film stock: Public Record Office, Home Office Papers (hereafter PRO–HO) 45/10624.

8 Cinematograph Act 1909 (9 Edw. 7 ch. 30), section 1.

9 Regulations dated 20 December 1909 made by the Secretary of State under the Cinematograph Act, 1909 (S.R. & O. 1909 no. 1465); recommendations of the LCC Theatres and Music Halls Committee, 21 December 1909, cited by Hunnings, *Film Censors and the Law*, p. 46.

10 London County Council v. Bermondsey Bioscope Co. Ltd [1911] 1 KB 445.

11 Theatre de Luxe (Halifax) Ltd v. Gledhill [1915] 2 KB 49. For details of other cases brought under the Cinematograph Act, see Hunnings, *Film Censors and the Law*, pp. 85–9.

12 Obscene Publications Act 1857 (20 & 21 Vict. ch. 83); Law Commission, *Criminal Law: Report on Conspiracy and Criminal Law Reform*, Law Comm. no. 76 (London: HMSO, 1976). No prosecutions of publicly exhibited films for indecency or obscenity have been traced in the period covered by this inquiry.

13 Ellis v. Dubowksi [1921] 3 KB 621.

14 Mills v. London County Council [1925] 1 KB 213.

15 T. C. Hartley and J. A. G. Griffith, *Government and Law* (London: Weidenfeld & Nicolson, 1981). The distinction between 'administrative' and 'legislative' is difficult to maintain in practice, however: see J. A. G. Griffith and H. Street, *Principles of Administrative Law*, 5th ed. (London: Pitman, 1973), p. 56; and the discussion in chapter 7 of this book.

16 PRO–HO 158/18, 'Cinematograph licences: model conditions', circular 312,397/151, 24 January 1917; 158/23, 'The censorship of cinematograph films', circular 373,422/78, 6 July 1923. Full texts of both circulars are reproduced in Annette Kuhn, 'Censorship, Sexuality and the Regulation of Cinema, 1909–1925' (PhD thesis, University of London, 1986), Appendix.

17 Hunnings, *Film Censors and the Law*, p. 82.

18 Hunnings, *Film Censors and the Law*, p. 16.

19 PRO–HO 45/10551, notes on a deputation, 22 February 1912.

20 PRO–HO 45/10551, 'Re Censorship of Kinematograph Films', document presented by a deputation to the Home Office, 13 November 1912.

21 PRO–HO 45/10551, BBFC circular, January 1913; BBFC, *Annual Report 1913*.

22 Figures on local authorities' acceptance of the BBFC's rulings are taken from Robertson, *The British Board of Film Censors*, p. 7. PRO–HO 45/10551 contains correspondence received by the Home Office calling for official censorship.

23 PRO–HO 158/17, circular 264,149, 16 May 1916. See Kuhn, 'Censorship, Sexuality and the Regulation of Cinema', Appendix, for the full text of this circular.

24 An account of the film trade's dissatisfaction with censorship arrangements appears in Rachael Low, *The History of the British Film, 1914–1918* (London: Allen & Unwin, 1950), pp. 126–34.

25 PRO–HO 45/10702, notes on a deputation from the CEA, April 1913; PRO–HO 45/10812, report of a deputation from the CEA, 26 May 1916; PRO–HO 45/10811, 'Censorship of Cinematograph Films', Cabinet memo, 3 October 1916.

26 PRO–HO 158/18, circular 312,397/151, 24 January 1917. Events leading up to the issue of this circular are discussed more fully in chapter 3. See also PRO–HO 158/18, circular 312,397/206a, amending the January circular.

27 Home Office records for 1921 suggest there was some disagreement on this issue within the department. One official, S. W. Harris (who in 1947 became BBFC president), was in favour of allowing the trade censorship to continue. Another, Sir Malcolm Delevigne, took a more cautious line ('the present position is not altogether satisfactory'). PRO–HO 45/11191, Home Office memo, dated 21 February 1921; Home Office comment on BBFC *Annual Report 1919*, dated 21 December 1921.

28 PRO–HO 158/21, circular 312,397/265, 3 November 1919; PRO–HO 45/11191, report on replies to November 1919 circular, December 1921.
29 Ellis v. Dubowski [1921] 3 KB 621. For Home Office involvement in the *Auction of Souls* affair, see PRO–HO 45/10955.
30 PRO–HO 45/11191, confidential memo by Cecil Levita, Chair of LCC Theatres and Music Halls Committee, 3 October 1921; notes on a visit to Home Office by Levita, 26 October 1921; Home Office memos dated 21 October 1921 and 27 October 1921. BBFC, *Annual Report 1921*; Hunnings, *Film Censors and the Law*, pp. 73–4.
31 *The Times*, 2 February 1922; 11 March 1922; 1 April 1922; 22 May 1922; 30 December 1922; 19 January 1923.
32 PRO–HO 45/11191, notes on a conference at the Home Office, 2 May 1923.
33 PRO–HO 158/23, 'The Censorship of Cinematograph Films', circular 373,422/78, 6 July 1923. See Kuhn, 'Censorship, Sexuality and the Regulation of Cinema', Appendix, for the full text of this circular.
34 PRO–HO 45/22906, report on adoption of 1923 conditions, June 1924; *Justice of the Peace*, 21 June 1924, p. 377; Mills v. London County Council [1925] 1 KB 213.

3 The Morale of the Race and the Amusement of the Public

1 Anthony Slide, *Early Women Directors: Their Role in the Development of the Silent Cinema* (New York: A. S. Barnes & Co., 1977), chapter 2; see also Anthony Slide, 'Restoring "The Blot" ', *American Film* 1, 1 (1975), pp. 71–2.
2 David M. Kennedy, *Birth Control in America: The Career of Margaret Sanger* (New Haven: Yale University Press, 1970), chapter 3. *Birth Control*, a film by Margaret Sanger, was banned by the New York City license commissioner in 1917: see Edward de Grazia and Roger K. Newman, *Banned Films: Movies, Censors and the First Amendment* (New York: R. R. Bowker, 1982), pp. 186–8.
3 *Variety*, 14 April 1916, p. 26.
4 'U Film's Big Business', *Variety*, 21 April 1916, p. 25; *Exhibitors Herald*, 13 May 1916, p. 15; advertisement for states' rights, *Variety*, 16 June 1916, p. 23.
5 *Variety*, 14 April 1916, p. 26; *New York Dramatic Mirror*, 22 April 1916, p. 42, reprinted in Anthony Slide, *Selected Film Criticism, 1912–1920* (Metuchen, NJ: Scarecrow Press, 1982), pp. 279–80; *Moving Picture World*, 29 April 1916, pp. 817–18; *Photoplay*, June 1916, p. 95.
6 Mutual Film Corp. v. Industrial Commission of Ohio [1915] 236 US 230; Ira H. Carmen, *Movies, Censorship and the Law* (Ann Arbor: University of Michigan Press, 1966), pp. 10–16; Richard S. Randall, *Censorship of the Movies* (Madison: University of Wisconsin Press, 1968), pp. 18–25.
7 *Variety*, 14 April 1916, p. 26. This practice was of 'dubious legality', according to de Grazia and Newman, *Banned Films*, p. 188. On film censorship in New York City at this period, see Daniel Czitrom, 'The redemption of leisure: the National Board of Censorship and the rise of motion pictures in New York City, 1900–1920', *Studies in Visual Communication* 10, 4 (1984), pp. 2–6.
8 *New York Times*, 18 June 1916, section 8, p. 3; *Moving Picture World*, 1 July 1916, p. 73.
9 Neville March Hunnings, *Film Censors and the Law* (London: Allen & Unwin, 1967), pp. 160–61.
10 *Variety*, 7 July 1916, p. 22.
11 *Motion Picture News*, 7 October 1916, pp. 2206, 2208. The Pennsylvania Censor

explains his views on cinema in Ellis Paxson Oberholtzer, *The Morals of the Movie* (Philadelphia: Penn Publishing Co., 1922).

12 Louise Heck-Rabi, *Women Filmmakers: A Critical Reception* (Metuchen, NJ: Scarecrow Press, 1984), p. 58.

13 *Variety*, 14 April 1916, p. 26.

14 David Bordwell, Janet Staiger and Kristin Thompson, *The Classical Hollywood Cinema: Film Style and Mode of Production to 1960* (London: Routledge & Kegan Paul, 1985), chapter 14.

15 Discussion herein is based on the print of *Where Are My Children* held in the Motion Picture, Broadcasting and Recorded Sound Division of the Library of Congress. This print is incomplete, but I have reconstructed the narrative of the missing section from the Library of Congress copyright entry for the film. No print of the British version appears to have survived.

16 G. R. Searle, *Eugenics and Politics in Britain, 1900–1914* (Leyden: Noordhoff International Publishing, 1976), p. 39; see also Jeffrey Weeks, *Sex, Politics and Society: The Regulation of Sexuality since 1800* (London: Longman, 1981), chapter 7.

17 C. W. Saleeby, *Woman and Womanhood: A Search for Principles* (London: Heinemann, 1912), p. 25. In the US at this time, it was widely believed that abortion had become 'the "systematic" practice of "respectable" women – those who were married, middle- or upper-middle-class, native-born Protestants': Rosalind Pollack Petchesky, *Abortion and Woman's Choice* (New York: Longman, 1984), p. 78. The 'maternalism' of some British versions of eugenics is discussed by Anna Davin in 'Imperialism and motherhood', *History Workshop Journal*, 5 (1978), pp. 9–65; and by Lucy Bland in ' "Guardians of the race" or "Vampires upon the nation's health"? Female sexuality and its regulation in early twentieth century Britain', in *The Changing Experience of Women*, edited by Elizabeth Whitelegg et al. (Oxford: Basil Blackwell, 1982), pp. 373–88.

18 Edward Branigan, 'Formal permutations of the point-of-view shot', *Screen* 16, 3 (1975), pp. 54–64.

19 Laura Mulvey, 'Visual pleasure and narrative cinema', *Screen* 16, 3 (1975), pp. 6–18.

20 Searle, *Eugenics and Politics in Britain*, p. 59.

21 Bordwell, Staiger and Thompson, *The Classical Hollywood Cinema*, part 1.

22 Sections of the prewar women's movement had campaigned against marriage: see Havelock Ellis, *Sex in Relation to Society*, Studies in the Psychology of Sex, vol. 6 (Philadelphia: F. A. Davis, 1910), pp. 3–4; Sheila Jeffreys, ' "Free from all uninvited touch of man": women's campaigns around sexuality, 1880–1914', in *The Sexuality Papers*, by Lal Coveney et al. (London: Hutchinson, 1984), pp. 22–44 (pp. 40–43).

23 Edward J. Bristow, *Vice and Vigilance: Purity Movements in Britain since 1700* (Dublin: Gill & Macmillan, 1977), pp. 144–5; *The Times*, 31 May 1911, p. 5d. On the social purity movement in general, see Weeks, *Sex, Politics and Society*, chapters 5 and 11.

24 National Council of Public Morals, National Birth-Rate Commission, *The Declining Birth-Rates: Its Causes and Effects*, 2nd ed. (London: Chapman & Hall, 1917), p. 78. Earlier studies on the subject include Sidney Webb, *The Decline in the Birth Rate*, Fabian Tract no. 131 (London: Fabian Society, 1907).

25 *The Bioscope*, 9 November 1916, p. 561; *The Times*, 1 November 1916, p. 5b; James Marchant, quoted in *The Bioscope*, 9 November 1916, p. 561.

26 Public Record Office, Home Office Papers (hereafter PRO–HO) 45/10955, Home Office memo on *Where Are My Children*, dated 14 April 1917.

27 *The Cinema*, 16 November 1916, p. 3. The event is also reported in *Kinematograph and Lantern Weekly*, 9 November 1916, pp. 14–15; and in *The Bioscope*, 16 November 1916, p. 631.

28 *The Bioscope*, 16 November 1916, p. 631; 23 November 1916, p. 743; PRO–HO 45/10955, ' "Where Are My Children": Special Propaganda Film – Some Leading Opinions', NCPM promotional leaflet.

29 PRO–HO 158/17, circular 264,149, 16 May 1916. PRO–HO 45/10812, Home Office minute, dated 11 July 1923; PRO–HO 45/10811, 'Censorship of cinematograph films', Cabinet memo, 3 October 1916.

30 The many trade press reports and editorials on the campaign include: *The Cinema*, 2 November 1916, pp. 2–3; *Kinematograph and Lantern Weekly*, 9 November 1916, pp. 8–9; *The Bioscope*, 9 November 1916, pp. 536–7; *The Cinema*, 16 November 1916, p. 2.

31 *The Times*, 29 November 1916; *The Bioscope*, 30 November 1916, p. 845; PRO–HO 45/10811, James Marchant to Home Office, 27 November 1916.

32 PRO–HO 45/10811, handwritten minute, dated 29 December 1916; memo on visit by T. P. O'Connor to Home Office, dated 3 January 1917.

33 PRO–HO 158/18, 'Cinematograph Licences: Model Conditions', circular 312, 397/ 151, 24 January 1917; *The Bioscope*, 1 February 1917, p. 421; *Ex p*. Stott [1916] 1 KB 7. The full text of the circular is reproduced in Annette Kuhn, 'Censorship, Sexuality and the Regulation of Cinema, 1909–1925' (PhD thesis, University of London, 1986), Appendix.

34 PRO–HO 45/10955, T. P. O'Connor to Home Secretary, 27 March 1917.

35 PRO–HO 45/10955, Home Office memo on *Where Are My Children*, dated 14 April 1917.

36 National Council of Public Morals, Commission of Inquiry on Cinema, *The Cinema: Its Present Position and Future Possibilities* (London: Williams & Norgate, 1917), p. 2. Special (i.e. non-theatrical) screenings of *Where Are My Children* are reported in Birmingham in May (*The Times*, 1 May 1917, p. 3c) and during National Baby Week in July (*The Times*, 1 May 1917, p. 9c). No record has been found of any commercial screenings of the film in Britain.

37 John Hill, 'The British "social problem" film: *Violent Playground* and *Sapphire*', *Screen* 26, 1 (1985), pp. 34–48 (p. 35).

38 Institutional structures of non-commercial, but public, exhibition did not come into existence in Britain until the late 1920s, with the formation of the Film Society. This development, significantly, coincides with the invention of the concept of documentary cinema, with its suggestion of non-fictional form combined with educative purpose.

4 A Moral Subject

1 On narrative structure in general, see Vladimir Propp, *Morphology of the Folktale*, 2nd ed. (Austin: University of Texas Press, 1968); Roland Barthes, 'Introduction to the structural analysis of narratives', in *Image-Music-Text* (London: Fontana/Collins, 1977), pp. 79–124. On classical narrative structure in cinema, see David Bordwell and Kristin Thompson, *Film Art: An Introduction* (Reading, MA: Addison-Wesley, 1979), chapter 3. Descriptions of films in this chapter are based in part upon viewings made possible by the National Film Archive, by the Motion Picture, Broadcasting and Recorded Sound Division of the Library of Congress, and by David Samuelson. See 'Sources Consulted: Films' for further details.

2 Library of Congress, Motion Picture, Broadcasting and Recorded Sound Division, Copyright Deposit Material (hereafter LC-CM), L13765, synopsis of *Open Your Eyes*, 18 May 1919; *Kinematograph Weekly*, 22 January 1920, p. 119.

3 Quoted passages referring to *Fit to Fight* and *The End of the Road* are drawn from synopses of the films in Fawcett Library, National Vigilance Association Records (hereafter FL-NVA), S1[3].

4 LC-CM, L14184, script of *The End of the Road*, 1 March 1919.

5 Bill Nichols, 'Documentary theory and practice', *Screen* 17, 4 (1976/7), pp. 34–48; Annette Kuhn, 'The camera I: observations on documentary', *Screen* 19, 2 (1978), pp. 71–84. Silent films, of course, would have no incorporated voice-over, though the notion of a 'lecture film' does imply an authoritative voice – precisely that of a lecturer. On the role of the 'lecturer' in silent cinema, see Noel Burch, 'How we got into pictures: notes accompanying *Correction Please*', *Afterimage*, 8–9 (1981), pp. 22–38.

6 Bordwell and Thompson, *Film Art: An Introduction*, pp. 163–73, Barry Salt, *Film Style and Technology: History and Analysis* (London: Starword, 1983), pp. 162–5; David Bordwell, Janet Staiger and Kristin Thompson, *The Classical Hollywood Cinema: Film Style and Mode of Production to 1960* (London: Routledge & Kegan Paul, 1985), chapter 14.

7 Rachael Low, *The History of the British Film, 1918–1929* (London: Allen & Unwin, 1971), p. 141.

8 Burch, 'How we got into pictures'.

9 Stephen Heath, *Questions of Cinema* (London: Macmillan, 1981), chapter 4.

10 On the latter, see Lucy Bland and Frank Mort, 'Look out for the "good time" girl: dangerous sexualities as threat to national health', in *Formations of Nation and People* (London: Routledge & Kegan Paul, 1984), pp. 131–51; and chapters 3 and 6 of this book.

11 *Kinematograph Weekly*, 25 December 1919, p. 63.

12 *The Times*, 8 November 1919, p. 15e; *The Shield*, December 1919–January 1920, pp. 189–90; *Kinematograph Weekly*, 22 January 1920, p. 119.

13 *Kinematograph Weekly*, 25 December 1919, p. 70.

14 On the NCCVD, see Edward J. Bristow, *Vice and Vigilance: Purity Movements in Britain Since 1700* (Dublin: Gill & Macmillan, 1977), p. 149. On the Royal Commission on Venereal Diseases, see Jeffrey Weeks, *Sex, Politics and Society: The Regulation of Sexuality Since 1800* (London: Longman, 1981), p. 215.

15 Public Record Office, Home Office Papers (hereafter PRO–HO), 45/10955, Lord Sydenham to Sir George Cave, 6 August 1917.

16 On *Open Your Eyes*, for example, see *Kinematograph Weekly*, 22 January 1920, p. 119.

17 British Board of Film Censors, *Annual Report 1919*; 'Film censorship and health propaganda', *Bioscope*, 18 December 1919, p. 89.

18 PRO–HO 45/10955, handwritten minute, 14 August 1917.

19 *The Times*, 11 November 1919, p. 11d; 5 January 1920, p. 10a.

20 Neville March Hunnings, *Film Censors and the Law* (London: Allen & Unwin, 1967), p. 71; *Bioscope*, 6 February 1919, p. 51.

21 *The Cinema*, 16 December 1920; Low, *History of the British Film, 1918–1929*, p. 61.

22 Dorothy Knowles; *The Censor, the Drama and the Film, 1900–1934* (London: Allen & Unwin, 1934), p. 244.

23 *The Shield*, December 1919–January 1920, p. 190.

24 FL–NVA, S1[E], 'Conditions under which propaganda films may be exhibited at premises licensed by the Council', London County Council, March 1926.

25 Ivor Montagu, 'The censorship of sex in films', in *Proceedings of the Third Congress of the World League for Sexual Reform, 1929* (London: Kegan Paul, Trench & Trubner, 1930), p. 330.

26 Material quoted in this paragraph is from FL–NVA, S1³, 'Memorandum on the use of Social Hygiene propaganda films in the United States', 1932.

27 Karl S. Lashley and John B. Watson, *A Psychological Study of Motion Pictures in Relation to Venereal Disease Campaigns* (Washington, DC: US Interdepartmental Social Hygiene Board, 1922).

28 *Vigilance Record*, November 1931, p. 41.

29 Academy of Motion Picture Acts and Sciences, Production Code Administration Case Files, *Damaged Goods* (a.k.a. *Marriage Forbidden*) etc., 1927–40; *Damaged Lives*, 1933–53; FL–NVA, S1⁶, *Marriage Forbidden*.

30 United Kingdom, Royal Commission on Venereal Diseases, *Final Report of the Commissioners*, Cd. 8189 (London: HMSO, 1916), para. 232.

31 Bland and Mort, 'Look out for the "good time" girl. . .'. On the moral significance of the 'scourge' of syphilis, see Susan Sontag, *Illness as Metaphor* (New York: Random House, 1979), p. 39.

32 Royal Commission on Venereal Diseases, *Final Report*, para. 236.

33 Michel Foucault, *The History of Sexuality, Volume One: An Introduction* (New York: Pantheon Books, 1978), p. 122.

5 Pleasure, Prevention and Productivity

1 Jeffrey Weeks, *Sex, Politics and Society: The Regulation of Sexuality Since 1800* (London: Longman, 1981), chapter 10; Sheila Rowbotham, *Hidden from History* (London: Pluto Press, 1973), p. 150; Jane Lewis, 'The ideology and politics of birth control in interwar England', *Women's Studies International Quarterly* 2 (1979), pp. 33–48; Robert E. Dowse and John Peel, 'The politics of birth control', *Political Studies* 13 (1965), pp. 179–97.

2 British Library, Marie Stopes Collection (hereafter BL–SC) ADD 58507, memo of meeting with producers of film, dated 11 April 1923. For biographical information on Stopes, see Ruth Hall, *Marie Stopes: A Biography* (London: Andre Deutsch, 1977).

3 Ruth Hall, ed., *Dear Dr Stopes: Sex in the 1920s* (Harmondsworth: Penguin, 1981).

4 Weeks, *Sex, Politics and Society*, p. 192; Lewis, 'The ideology and politics of birth control', pp. 35–8.

5 Muriel Box, ed., *The Trial of Marie Stopes* (London: Femina Books, 1967); Hall, *Marie Stopes*, chapter 13.

6 Hall, *Marie Stopes*, p. 243; Marie Carmichael Stopes, *Married Love: A New Contribution to the Solution of Sex Difficulties*, 11th ed. (London: G. P. Putnam's Sons Ltd, 1923).

7 *Daily Telegraph*, 14 May 1923.

8 *Bioscope*, 17 May 1923, p. 61; *Kinematograph Weekly*, 17 May 1923, p. 73.

9 Leader, *Kinematograph Weekly*, 17 May 1923, p. 59.

10 BL–SC ADD 58507, BBFC to Napoleon Films, 11 May 1923.

11 British Board of Film Censors, *Annual Report 1923*. Other book-based films which ran into censorship trouble at this time include *Three Weeks*, a Sam Goldwyn production founded on a racy Elinor Glyn novel, and *La Garçonne*, based on a book by French writer Victor Margueritte which was banned in

Britain: Public Record Office, Home Office Papers (hereafter PRO–HO) 45/20045; PRO–HO 45/11446.

12 PRO–HO 45/11382, Home Office memo, dated 24 May 1923.

13 BL–SC ADD 58507, Napoleon Films to Marie Stopes (MCS), 14 May 1923; MCS to T. P. O'Connor, 15 May 1923.

14 PRO–HO 45/11382, Home Office memo, dated 24 May 1923.

15 PRO–HO 158/23, 'The censorship of cinematograph films', circular 373,422/78, 6 July 1923: for the full text of this circular, see Annette Kuhn, 'Censorship, Sexuality and the Regulation of Cinema, 1909–1925' (PhD thesis, University of London, 1986), Appendix. See also PRO–HO 45/11191 and 45/22906.

16 PRO–HO 45/11382, Home Office memo, dated 24 May 1923.

17 Neville March Hunnings, 'T. P. O'Connor's 43 rules', in *Film Censors and the Law* (London: Allen & Unwin, 1967), pp. 408–9.

18 BL–SC ADD 58507, Brooke Wilkinson to Napoleon Films, 29 May 1923.

19 BL–SC ADD 58507, Napoleon Films to MCS, 2 July 1923. The amendments agreed were:

a Opening intertitle – 'Camberwell' changed to Slumland'
b 'Can't you work that damned thing in the daytime?' to 'Can't you work that machine in the daytime?'
c 'It's drudgery and then it will be children, children, and we can't afford to clothe and keep them' to 'It's drudgery, drudgery from morning till night'
d Delete 'Your father died before he did the harm mine's done'
e 'Did I ask to be created? Don't you think had I known I should have remained unborn?' to 'I almost wish I had never been born'
f 'Afraid to make another home' to '. . . have another home'
g Change 'I wish to say goodnight to Amelia's children'.

In the version of the film discussed in this chapter, only amendments a, b, d and e have been effected.

20 London County Council, Music Halls and Theatres Committee, 27 June 1923; BL–SC ADD 58507, Napoleon Films to MCS, 20 June 1923; LCC to Napoleon Films, 3 July 1923; LCC to various London cinemas, June and July 1923; LCC to MCS, 16 July 1923.

21 PRO–HO 45/11382, Brooke Wilkinson to Home Office, 27 June 1923. It should be noted that *Maisie's Marriage* was released only a few months after the implementation of the LCC's controversial regulation excluding unaccompanied children from screenings of 'A' films (chapter 2). The film's 'A' certificate would therefore – at least in the populous LCC area – have greatly limited its audience.

22 PRO–HO 45/11382, handwritten Home Office minute, dated 28 June 1923; BL–SC ADD 58507, correspondence between BBFC and Napoleon Films, 22, 25 and 27 June 1923; *Daily Herald*, 28 June 1923.

23 BL–SC ADD 58507, Cinematograph Exhibitors' Association to MCS, 6 June 1923; *Kinematograph Weekly*, 7 June 1923, p. 61; 21 June 1923, p. 51.

24 *Morning Post*, 11 July 1923; BL–SC ADD 58507, correspondence between MCS and Chief Constables, July 1923; Frederick White to MCS, 9 August 1923. It is difficult to assess the validity of the distributor's claim that all deleted parts of the film had been restored: it may well have been made in order to placate Stopes.

25 PRO–HO 45/11382, minute by S. W. Harris, dated 27 June 1923.

26 PRO–HO 45/11382, circular 446,368/3, 30 June 1923: this circular is reproduced in Kuhn, 'Censorship, Sexuality and the Regulation of Cinema', Appendix.

27 Hall, *Marie Stopes*, p. 245, footnote quoting a local newspaper advertisement for

Maisie's Marriage, 21 July 1923; PRO–HO 45/11382, correspondence between Home Office and Sheffield Chief Constable, July and August 1923.

28 PRO–HO 45/11382, MCS to Home Office, 11 July 1923; Home Office to MCS, 12 July 1923; BL–SC ADD 58507, MCS to Home Office, 14 July 1923; Home Office to MCS, 17 July 1923.

29 Hall, *Marie Stopes*, p. 245.

30 All references to *Maisie's Marriage* herein are based on the print of the film in possession of the Samuelson family, which was loaned to the author by David Samuelson. This print has a Censor's certificate which is placed *after* the title card.

31 This approach is based upon the structural analysis of narrative. See, for example, Vladimir Propp, *Morphology of the Folktale*, 2nd ed. (Austin: University of Texas Press, 1968).

32 Marie Carmichael Stopes, *Wise Parenthood: The Treatise on Birth Control for Married People*, 10th ed. (London: G. P. Putnam's Sons Ltd, 1922), chapter 1.

33 Stopes, *Married Love*, chapter 5.

34 For example, the scene in the nightclub recalls Stopes's contention that if married couples cultivated an enjoyment of sex, husbands would have neither the need nor the desire to resort to prostitutes (*Married Love*, chapter 3). And a scene in which the Sterling children are told that their cat is pregnant evokes the argument that parents should be frank with children on sexual matters (Marie Carmichael Stopes, *Radiant Motherhood: A Book for Those Who Are Creating the Future* [London: G. P. Putnam's Sons Ltd, 1925], chapter 18).

35 'The half-swooning sense of flux which overtakes the spirit in that eternal moment at the apex of rapture, sweeps into its flaming tides the whole essence of man and woman. . . .' (Stopes, *Married Love*, p. 130). This is by no means untypical.

36 Dowse and Peel, 'The politics of birth control'.

37 This is a distinction made in auteur-structuralist film theory. Stopes – regarded as 'author', an individual, the creative subjectivity behind the film to which her name is attached – is to be seen as distinct from 'Stopes', a convenient label for a structural element of the film which is not reducible to the input or conscious intent of Stopes the person. See Peter Wollen, *Signs and Meaning in the Cinema*, 3rd ed. (London: Secker & Warburg, 1972), pp. 167–8.

38 The distinction is proposed by Tzvetan Todorov, 'Categories of the literary narrative', *Film Reader*, 2 (1977), pp. 19–37; see also Annette Kuhn, *Women's Pictures: Feminism and Cinema* (London: Routledge & Kegan Paul, 1982), p. 52.

39 On Stopes's protest to the Home Office that attempts were being made to delete her name from the film, S. W. Harris expressed the private opinion that 'I never imagined this could be part of the undertaking (desirable as it might be!)': PRO–HO 45/11382, handwritten Home Office minute, dated 12 July 1923.

40 Margaret Dickinson and Sarah Street, *Cinema and the State: The Film Industry and the British Government, 1927–84* (London: British Film Institute, 1985), pp. 8–12. See also chapter 2 of this book.

6 Sexuality and the Cinema

1 Jeffrey Weeks, *Sexuality and its Discontents: Meanings, Myths and Modern Sexualities* (London: Routledge & Kegan Paul, 1985), p. 7.

2 Nikolas Rose, 'The psychological complex: mental measurement and social administration', *Ideology and Consciousness*, 5 (1979), pp. 5–68.

3 G. R. Searle, *Eugenics and Politics in Britain, 1900–1914* (Leyden: Noordhoff International Publishing, 1976).

4 Weeks, *Sexuality and its Discontents*, chapter 4.

5 Weeks, *Sexuality and its Discontents*, p. 70.

6 On 'expert' advice about sexual matters, see Ellen Ross, ' "The love crisis": couples' advice books of the late 1970s', in *Women, Sex and Sexuality*, edited by Catharine R. Stimpson and Ethel Spector Person (Chicago: University of Chicago Press, 1980), pp. 274–87 (p. 279). For a radical feminist view of these developments, see Sheila Jeffreys, 'Sex reform and anti-feminism in the 1920s', in *The Sexual Dynamics of History*, edited by the London Feminist History Group (London: Pluto Press, 1983), pp. 177–202.

7 C. Fraser Brockington, *A Short History of Public Health* (London: J. and A. Churchill Ltd, 1966), p. 53.

8 Havelock Ellis, *The Task of Social Hygiene* (London: Constable & Co. Ltd, 1912), p. 1.

9 Edward J. Bristow, *Vice and Vigilance: Purity Movements in Britain Since 1700* (Dublin: Gill and Macmillan, 1977); Jeffrey Weeks, *Sex, Politics and Society: The Regulation of Sexuality Since 1800* (London: Longman, 1981), chapter 5.

10 For example, signatories to the NCPM's manifesto included representatives of various churches and religious bodies, ranging from six bishops to 'General' William Booth of the Salvation Army; academics and practitioners in the fields of science, medicine, eugenics and philosophy; politicians; and public figures such as Beatrice Webb, Mary Scharlieb, C. W. Saleeby and Rider Haggard: *The Times*, 31 May 1911, p. 5d.

11 Michael Freeden, 'Eugenics and progressive thought: a study in ideological affinity', *Historical Journal* 22 (1979), pp. 645–71.

12 See Sheila Rowbotham, *Hidden from History* (London: Pluto Press, 1978), chapter 22; Jane Lewis, 'The ideology and politics of birth control in interwar England', *Women's Studies International Quarterly* 2 (1979), pp. 33–48.

13 On the denigration of one form of knowledge, folk 'science', see Carlo Ginzburg, 'Morelli, Freud and Sherlock Holmes: clues and the scientific method', *History Workshop Journal*, 9 (1980), pp. 5–36.

14 In 1917, following a recommendation of the Royal Commission on Venereal Diseases, Parliament passed the Venereal Diseases Act, which placed restrictions upon advertising and practice by unqualified practitioners.

15 As Edward Bristow suggests: see *Vice and Vigilance*, pp. 149–51.

7 A New Public Sphere

1 H. L. A. Hart, *Law, Liberty and Morality* (London: Oxford University Press, 1963), p. 4; Patrick Devlin, *The Enforcement of Morals* (London: Oxford University Press, 1965). On public and private, see Beverly Brown, 'Private faces in public places', *Ideology and Consciousness*, 7 (1980), pp. 3–16.

2 This phrase forms part of the first of the recommended licensing conditions as set out by the Home Office in its January 1917 circular: Public Record Office, Home Office papers (hereafter PRO-HO) 158/18, 'Cinematograph licences: model conditions', circular 312,397/151, 24 January 1917. For the complete text of this circular, see Annette Kuhn, 'Censorship, Sexuality and the Regulation of Cinema, 1909–1925' (PhD thesis, University of London, 1986), Appendix.

3 T. C. Hartley and J. A. G. Griffith, *Government and Law* (London: Weidenfeld & Nicolson, 1981).

4 J. A. G. Griffith and H. Street, *Principles of Administrative Law*, 5th ed. (London: Pitman, 1973), p. 57.

5 See Miriam Hansen, 'Early silent cinema: whose public sphere?' *New German Critique*, 29 (1983), pp. 147–84.

6 PRO–HO 45/10955, handwritten minute, 14 August 1917.

7 National Council of Public Morals, Cinema Commission of Inquiry, *The Cinema: Its Present Position and Future Possibilities* (London: Williams & Norgate, 1917), p. xxvi; PRO–HO 45/24570, Reports on improper behaviour in cinemas; PRO–HO 45/12969, Memo on children and the cinema, July 1925. The inclusion in the 1917 model conditions of a clause relating to lighting was a direct outcome of these concerns.

8 PRO–HO 45/11008, Report of Bradford MOH, 1917.

9 *The Times*, 5 January 1915. See also PRO–HO 45/11008, report on a deputation of educationists, 29 May 1916; and the objectives, noted later in this chapter, of the Cinema Commission of Inquiry.

10 PRO–HO 158/17, circular 264,149, 16 May 1916. For the full text of this letter, see Kuhn, 'Censorship, Sexuality and the Regulation of Cinema', Appendix.

11 In 'Early silent cinema', Miriam Hansen argues that in Germany the gender composition of audiences was crucial in the production of a public sphere of cinema there. This does not appear to have been the case in Britain.

12 *The Times*, 29 November 1916; National Council of Public Morals, *The Cinema*, p. ix. Michel Foucault's discussion of 'pastoral power' in the twentieth century is illuminating in this context. He argues that the objective of power shifts away from that salvation in the next world which is associated with religious forms of pastoral power, and moves towards a this-worldly concept of salvation seen in terms of 'health, well-being . . ., security, protection against accidents': 'The subject and power', *Critical Inquiry* 8 (1982), pp. 777–95 (p. 784).

13 Jeffrey Richards, *The Age of the Dream Palace: Cinema and Society in Britain, 1930–1939* (London: Routledge & Kegan Paul, 1984), chapter 5.

14 *The Bioscope*, 12 April 1917, p. 103. This is typical of views widely expressed in the trade press of the period.

8 Rethinking Film Censorship

1 The relationship between social audience and spectator is explored by Annette Kuhn in 'Women's genres', *Screen* 25, 1 (1984), pp. 18–28.

2 T. P. O'Connor's 43 rules', in Neville March Hunnings, *Film Censors and the Law* (London: Allen & Unwin, 1967), pp. 408–9.

3 As early as 1915, the US Supreme Court ruled that cinema was not entitled to the protection from censorship accorded other publications under the First Amendment to the Constitution. Although this ruling was rescinded in 1952, cinema continued until very recently to be set apart from other cultural products in debates on censorship. In Britain in 1979, for example, the Williams Report recommended the abandonment of nearly all legal prohibitions on obscene publications, an exception to this being film, which in the Committee's view demanded continuing controls, because of the peculiar power of the cinematic image. Mutual Film Corp. v. Industrial Commission of Ohio [1915] 236 US 230; United Kingdom, Home Office, *Report of the Committee on Obscenity and Film Censorship*, Cd. 7772 (London: HMSO, 1979), para. 12.10.

4 During the 1930s, the Public Morality Council was the most influential pressure group in the field of film censorship. More extreme moralist views, such as

those espoused by the Birmingham Cinema Inquiry Committee, met with some opposition, however: see Birmingham Cinema Inquiry Committee, *Influence of Cinema on Children, April 1930–May 1931* (Birmingham, BCIC, 1931); British Film Institute, BBFC Verbatim Reports, Report of a deputation to the Home Secretary, 6 April 1932.

Sources Consulted

Films

The titles listed below are of films consulted in the course of this inquiry. Films I have viewed have an asterisk beside the title (e.g. *Maisie's Marriage*): prints of the rest could not be traced, and may well not have survived. The following information is included, where available and in the order given, with each entry:

Title
Date (usually of first release)
Country of origin (c)
Production company or producer (prod)
Director (dir)
Synopsis (s)
Location of print, if found (loc)
Unpublished documentation (du)
Selected published documentation (dp)

Damaged Goods (1915)

(c) US (prod) American Film Manufacturing Co. Inc. (s) Film version, with the original cast, of the Broadway version of Eugène Brieux's play about syphilis in a bourgeois family (loc) paper print, Library of Congress (du) Library of Congress, Motion Picture, Broadcasting and Recorded Sound Division, Copyright Deposit Material (hereafter LC-CM), L3450 (dp) *Moving Picture World* 2 October 1916.

Damaged Goods (1919)

(c) GB (prod) G. B. Samuelson (dir) Alexander Butler (s) Adaptation of the play by Eugène Brieux about syphilis in a bourgeois family (loc) David Samuelson (du) Public Record Office, Home Office Papers (hereafter PRO–HO) 45/10955 (dp) *Variety*, 21 November 1919; *The Times*, 17 December 1919; *The Bioscope*, 25 December 1919; *The Cinema*, 16 December 1920.

Damaged Lives (1937)

(c) Canada (prod) Weldon Pictures Corp. (dir) Edgar G. Ulmer (s) An update of the *Damaged Goods* story (loc) Library of Congress (du) Fawcett Library, National Vigilance Association Records (hereafter FL–NVA), S1Q; LC–CM, LP4100; Academy of Motion Picture Arts and Sciences, Production Code Administration Case Files (hereafter AMPAS–PCA) (dp) Dorothy Knowles, *The Censor, the Drama and the Film*, pp. 243–4; *New York Times Film Reviews*, 14 June 1937.

Doctor Ehrlich's Magic Bullet (1939)

(c) US (prod) Warner Brothers (dir) William Dieterle (s) Biopic about the discoverer of salvarsan, the first known cure for syphilis (loc) Library of Congress (du) AMPAS –PCA; University of Southern California, Doheny Library, Warner Brothers Collection (dp) *Variety*, 2 February 1940; *Film Daily*, 2 February 1940.

The End of the Road (1918)

(c) US (prod) Public Health Films (dir) Edward H. Griffith (s) The lives of two young women, one of whom leads a decent life and embarks on a career as a nurse while the other falls into 'disgrace' and contracts a venereal disease (du) FL–NVA, S1[3]; LC–CM, L13333, L14184 (dp) *The Shield*, December 1919–January 1920, pp. 189–90; *The Times*, 8 November 1919.

Fit to Fight (1919)

(c) US (prod) American Social Hygiene Association/Public Health Films (dir) Edward H. Griffith (s) Of five young men drafted into the Army, only two get to the front: the rest fall victim to VD (du) FL–NVA, S1[3]; LC–CM, L13350 (dp) Kevin Brownlow, *The War, the West and the Wilderness* (London: Secker & Warburg, 1979), pp. 127–8.

Fit to Win (1919)

(c) US (prod) American Social Hygiene Association/Public Health Films (dir) Edward H. Griffith (s) *Fit to Fight* (q.v.), with epilogue added (du) FL–NVA, S1[3]; LC–CM, L14210 (dp) Karl S. Lashley and John B. Watson, *A Psychological Study of Motion Pictures in Relation to Venereal Disease Campaigns*; Edward de Grazia and Roger K. Newman, *Banned Films*, pp. 199–200.

Maisie's Marriage (1923)

(c) GB (original title: *Married Love*) (prod) G. B. Samuelson (dir) Alexander Butler (s) 'A fireman's fiancée, rejected by her father, becomes a maid and finds small families happier than larger ones' (loc) David Samuelson (du) PRO–HO 45/11382; British Library, Marie Stopes Collection, ADD 58507 (dp) *The Bioscope*, 17 May 1923; *Kinematograph Weekly*, 17 May 1923, 7 June 1923.

Marriage Forbidden (1938)

(c) US (US release title: *Damaged Goods*) (prod) Criterion Pictures Corp. (dir) Phil Stone (s) 'On the dangers of syphilis to society, and the havoc in a family if unchecked': based upon Brieux's play *Damaged Goods* (loc) National Film Archive (du) FL–NVA. S1[6]; LC–CM, LP8129; AMPAS–PCA (dp) *New York Times Film Reviews*, 16 July 1938; *Kinematograph Weekly*, 26 January 1939.

Open Your Eyes (1919)

(c) US (prod) Warner Brothers (dir) Gilbert P. Hamilton (s) Three young men decide to sow their wild oats, and all of them contract syphilis as a result (du) LC–CM, L13765 (dp) *Variety*, 4 July 1919; *Wid's Daily*, 6 July 1919; *Kinematograph Weekly*, 22 January 1920.

The Scarlet Trail (1918)

(c) US (dir) John S. Lawrence (s) A VD film with a social purity subplot, ending with the suicide of a syphilis victim (du) LC–CM, L13541 (dp) *New York Times Film Reviews*, 22 December 1918; *Variety*, 3 January 1919.

The Spreading Evil (1918)

(c) US (dir) James Keane (s) A thriller whose plot revolves around the search for a cure for syphilis (du) LC–CM, L13209 (dp) *Variety*, 22 November 1919; Lashley and Watson, *A Psychological Study of Motion Pictures* . . ., p. 6.

*Whatsoever a Man Soweth (1919?)

(c) GB (prod) Lord Beaverbrook (s) A drama about VD among soldiers (loc) Archive Film Agency.

*Where Are My Children (1916)

(c) US (prod) Universal (dir) Lois Weber (s) An upper-middle-class woman has abortions and procures them for others, with disastrous consequences (loc) Library of Congress (du) PRO–HO 45/10955; LC–CM, L8170 (dp) *Variety*, 14 April 1916; *Moving Picture World*, 29 April 1916, 3 June 1916, 1 July 1916; *Photoplay*, June 1916; *The Bioscope*, 9 November 1916, 16 November 1916, 23 November 1916.

Unpublished documents

London. British Film Institute. Information Department. British Board of Film Censors. Verbatim Reports, 1930–35.
London. British Library. Department of Manuscripts. Marie Stopes Collection.
London. City of London Polytechnic. Fawcett Library. National Vigilance Association Papers, class S1 (films).
London. Public Record Office. Home Office Papers, classes HO45 and HO158.
Los Angeles, CA. Academy of Motion Picture Arts and Sciences. Margaret Herrick Library. Production Code Administration Case Files.
Los Angeles, CA. University of Southern California. Doheny Library. Warner Brothers Collection.
Washington, DC. Library of Congress. Motion Picture, Broadcasting and Recorded Sound Division. Film Copyright Deposit Material.

Contemporary published documents

(i) Journals and newspapers extensively consulted

THE BIOSCOPE
THE CINEMA
KINEMATOGRAPH WEEKLY
MOVING PICTURE WORLD (US)
THE TIMES
VARIETY (US)

(ii) Statute and case law

Ellis v. Dubowski [1921] 3 KB 621
London County Council v. Bermondsey Bioscope Co. Ltd [1911] 1 KB 445
Mills v. London County Council [1925] 1 KB 213
Mutual Film Corporation v. Industrial Commission of Ohio [1915] 236 US 230
Ex p. Stott [1916] 1 KB 7
Theatre de Luxe (Halifax) Ltd v. Gledhill [1915] 2 KB 49
UNITED KINGDOM. Laws. Statutes, etc. cinematograph Act, 1909, 9 Edw 7, ch. 30

(iii) Books, reports, official publications

BRIEUX, Eugène. Damaged Goods. 2nd ed. London: A. C. Fifield, 1917.
BRITISH BOARD OF FILM CENSORS. Annual Reports, 1913; 1919; 1925–36. London: British Board of Film Censors.
ELLIS, Havelock. Sex in Relation to Society. Studies in the Psychology of Sex, vol. 6. Philadelphia: F. A. Davis, 1910.
ELLIS, Havelock. The Task of Social Hygiene. London: Constable & Co. Ltd, 1912.
JOYNSON HICKS, William. Do We Need a Censor? London: Faber & Faber, 1929.
KNOWLES, Dorothy. The Censor, the Drama and the Film, 1900–1934. London: Allen & Unwin, 1934.
LASHLEY, Karl S., and WATSON, John B. A Psychological Study of Motion Pictures in Relation to Venereal Disease Campaigns. Washington, DC: US Interdepartmental Social Hygiene Board, 1922.
MONTAGU, Ivor. The Political Censorship of Films. London: Gollancz, 1939.
NATIONAL COUNCIL OF PUBLIC MORALS. Commission of Inquiry on Cinema. The Cinema: Its Present Position and Future Possibilities. London: Williams & Norgate, 1917.
NATIONAL COUNCIL OF PUBLIC MORALS. National Birth-Rate Commission. The Declining Birth-Rate: Its Causes and Effects. London: Chapman & Hall, 1917.
NATIONAL COUNCIL OF WOMEN OF GREAT BRITAIN. Cinema Committee. Report of an Enquiry into Film Censorship. London: National Council of Women, 1931.
PUBLIC MORALITY COUNCIL. Annual Reports, 1901–1913; 1929–38. London: Public Morality Council.
PUBLIC MORALITY COUNCIL. The Censorship of Films. London: Public Morality Council, 1930.
PUBLIC MORALITY COUNCIL. Report on Cinema Films. London: Public Morality Council, 1931.
SALEEBY, C. W. Woman and Womanhood: A Search for Principles. London: Heinemann, 1912.

STOPES, Marie Carmichael. *Married Love: A New Contribution to the Solution of Sex Difficulties*. 11th ed. London: G. P. Putnam's Sons Ltd, 1923.

STOPES, Marie Carmichael. *Radiant Motherhood: A Book for Those Who Are Creating the Future*. 4th ed. London: G. P. Putnam's Sons Ltd, 1925.

STOPES, Marie Carmichael. *Wise Parenthood: The Treatise on Birth Control for Married People*. 10th ed. London: G. P. Putnam's Sons Ltd, 1922.

UNITED KINGDOM. Home Office. *Children and 'A' Films*. Circular 596,323/20, 6 March 1933. London: HMSO, 1933.

UNITED KINGDOM. Home Office. *The Cinema and Children*. Circular 537,492/3, 16 December 1929. London: HMSO, 1931.

UNITED KINGDOM. Home Office. *Cinematograph Act 1909: Revision of Model Conditions*. Circular 676,417/6, 24 October 1934. London: HMSO, 1934.

UNITED KINGDOM. Royal Commission on Venereal Diseases. *Final Report of the Commissioners*. Cd. 8189. London: HMSO, 1916.

WORLD LEAGUE FOR SEXUAL REFORM. *Proceedings of the Third Congress, 1929*. London: Kegan Paul, Trench & Trubner, 1930.

Other published documents: A Selection

(i) Books

ALLEN, Robert C. and GOMERY, Douglas. *Film History: Theory and Practice*. New York: Alfred A. Knopf, 1985.

BETTS, Ernest. *The Film Business: A History of British Cinema, 1896–1972*. London: Allen & Unwin, 1973.

BORDWELL, David; STAIGER, Janet; and THOMPSON, Kristin, *The Classical Hollywood Cinema: Film Style and Mode of Production to 1960*. London: Routledge & Kegan Paul, 1985.

BRISTOW, Edward J. *Vice and Vigilance: Purity Movements in Britain Since 1700*. Dublin: Gill & Macmillan, 1977.

CARMEN, Ira H. *Movies, Censorship and the Law*. Ann Arbor: University of Michigan Press, 1966.

CURRAN, James, and PORTER, Vincent, eds. *British Cinema History*. London: Weidenfeld & Nicolson, 1983.

DE GRAZIA, Edward, and NEWMAN, Roger K. *Banned Films: Movies, Censors and the First Amendment*. New York: R. R. Bowker, 1982.

FOUCAULT, Michel. *Discipline and Punish: The Birth of the Prison*. Harmondsworth: Penguin, 1977.

FOUCAULT, Michel. *The History of Sexuality, Volume One: An Introduction*. New York: Pantheon Books, 1978.

FOUCAULT, Michel. *Language, Counter-Memory, Practice*. Oxford: Basil Blackwell, 1977.

FOUCAULT, Michel. *Power/Knowledge*. Brighton: Harvester Press, 1980.

HALL, Ruth, *Marie Stopes: A Biography*. London: Andre Deutsch, 1977.

HUNNINGS, Neville March. *Film Censors and the Law*. London: Allen & Unwin, 1967.

LONDON FEMINIST HISTORY GROUP *The Sexual Dynamics of History*. London: Pluto Press, 1983.

LOW, Rachael. *The History of the British Film, 1906–1914*. London: Allen & Unwin, 1949.

LOW, Rachael. *The History of the British Film, 1914–1918*. London: Allen & Unwin, 1950.
LOW, Rachael. *The History of the British Film, 1918–1929*. London: Allen & Unwin, 1971.
LOW, Rachael, and MANVELL, Roger. *The History of the British Film, 1896–1906*. London: Allen & Unwin, 1948.
PHELPS, Guy. *Film Censorship*. London: Gollancz, 1975.
PRONAY, Nicholas, and SPRING, D. W., eds. *Propaganda, Politics and Film, 1918–48*. London: Macmillan, 1982.
RANDALL, Richard S. *Censorship of the Movies*. Madison: University of Wisconsin Press, 1968.
ROBERTSON, James C. *The British Board of Film Censors: Film Censorship in Britain, 1896–1950*. London: Croom Helm, 1985.
SALT, Barry. *Film Style and Technology: History and Analysis*. London: Starword, 1983.
SEARLE, G. R. *Eugenics and Politics in Britain, 1900–1914*. Leyden: Noordhoff International Publishing, 1976.
SHORT, K. R. M., ed. *Feature Films as History*. London: Croom Helm, 1981.
SMITH, Paul, ed. *The Historian and Film*. Cambridge: Cambridge University Press, 1976.
THOMPSON, Kristin. *Exporting Entertainment: America in the World Film Market, 1907–34*. London: British Film Institute, 1985.
TREVELYAN, John. *What the Censor Saw*. London: Michael Joseph, 1973.
WEEKS, Jeffrey. *Sex, Politics and Society: The Regulation of Sexuality Since 1800*. London: Longman, 1981.
WEEKS, Jeffrey. *Sexuality and Its Discontents: Meanings, Myths and Modern Sexualities*. London: Routledge & Kegan Paul, 1985.
WHITE, Hayden. *Tropics of Discourse: Essays in Cultural Criticism*. Baltimore, MD: Johns Hopkins University Press, 1978.
YOUNG, Robert, ed. *Untying the Text: A Post-Structuralist Reader*. London: Routledge & Kegan Paul, 1981.

(ii) Articles

BLAND, Lucy, and MORT, Frank. 'Look out for the "good time" girl: dangerous sexualities as threat to national health', *Formations of Nation and People*. London: Routledge & Kegan Paul, 1984, pp. 131–51.
BURCH, Noel. 'How we got into pictures: notes accompanying *Correction Please*', *Afterimage*, 8–9 (1981), pp. 22–38.
FISHER, Robert. 'Film censorship and progressive reform: the National Board of Censorship of Motion Pictures, 1909–1922', *Journal of Popular Film*, 4 (1975), pp. 143–56.
FOUCAULT, Michel. 'Governmentality', *Ideology and Consciousness*, 6 (1979), pp. 5–21.
FOUCAULT, Michel. 'Questions of method', *Ideology and Consciousness*, 8 (1981), pp. 3–14.
FOUCAULT, Michel. 'The subject and power', *Critical Inquiry* 8 (1982), pp. 777–95.
FREEDEN, Michael. 'Eugenics and progressive thought: a study in ideological affinity', *Historical Journal* 22 (1979), pp. 645–71.
HANSEN, Miriam. 'Early silent cinema: whose public sphere?' *New German Critique*, 29 (1983), pp. 147–84.

LEWIS, Jane. 'The ideology and politics of birth control in interwar England', *Women's Studies International Quarterly* 2 (1979), pp. 33–48.

RICHARDS, Jeffrey. 'The British Board of Film Censors and content control in the 1930s: images of Britain', *Historical Journal of Film, Radio and TV* 1 (1981), pp. 95–116.

RICHARDS, Jeffrey. 'The British Board of Film Censors and content control in the 1930s: foreign affairs', *Historical Journal of Film, Radio and TV* 2 (1982), pp. 39–48.

SAID, Edward W. 'The problem of textuality: two exemplary positions', *Critical Inquiry* 4 (1978), pp. 673–714.

Index

abortion, 29–30, 32, 34–5
Aldred, Guy, 76
Allan, Robert C., 8
American Social Hygiene
  Association, 70
apparatus, 6–7
Association of Social and Moral
  Hygiene, 65
Auction of Souls, 25
audiences, cinema, 119–21,
  124–5, 129; and birth control,
  39, 92–3; class of, 112–13,
  120–2, 128–9; 'improvement'
  of, 122, 124, 132; and
  propaganda films, 37, 68–9,
  73–4

Bhaskar, Roy, 8
Bioscope, The, 39, 114
birth control, 29, 38–9, 76, 90,
  107; and cinema audiences,
  92–3; in *Maisie's Marriage*
  (*q.v.*), 75–96; in *Where Are My
  Children*, 30, 34–5; *see also*
  Stopes, Marie
Birth-Rate Commission, NCPM,
  38–9
Brieux, Eugène, 55
British Board of Film Censors
  (BBFC), 3, 21–7, 127, 132–3;
  code of, 129; and the Home
  Office, 24–7, 43–5, 79–80,
  132–3; legal status of, 19,
  118–19; and local authorities,
  19, 23, 25, 67, 70, 133; and
  Maisie's Marriage, 79–83, 90,
  94–6, 130; and propaganda
  films, 44–5, 66–70, 127, 130;
  and voluntary censorship, 14,

21–7; and *Where Are My
  Children*, 44–5, 47, 66
British Social Hygiene Council
  (BSHC), 72, 104, 106; before
  1925, *see* National Council for
  Combating Venereal Disease

causal analysis, 8
censorship, film: apparatus, 6–7;
  BBFC (*q.v.*), 21–7; and birth
  control, 75–96; institutions for,
  12–13; investigation of, 1–11;
  law and, 13–21; and power, 7–8,
  10–11, 131–4; and
  productivity, 95–6, 126–31;
  prohibition, 2–4, 126–31;
  public sphere, 114–25; and
  sexuality, 97–113; text and
  context, 4–8; and venereal
  disease propaganda, 49–74; and
  Where Are My Children, 29–48
certificates, BBFC, 22, 26
children, 36–7; film attendance,
  18, 22, 121
cinema, as public sphere, 114–25;
  contested, 117–24; *see also*
  audiences; censorship;
  exhibitors; film industry;
  narrative
Cinema Commission of Inquiry,
  BCPM, 43–6, 105, 120–3
cinemas, 13, 50, 117–19; licensing
  of, *see* local authorities; and
  morality, 38, 46, 69–74, 120–3
Cinematograph Act (1909), 1, 13;
  and the film industry, 14, 18;
  and the Home Office, 19–20;
  licences under, 16–19, 24; and
  public sphere for cinema, 47,
  116–18; and safety, 15–18, 20,